Sweeping Leaves
In The Wind

Darren Roberts

ISBN: 9798610607320

Cover picture:
By the author, Juno Beach, Normandy, France, 6th June 2019
All other pictures: Named

Lee served in 1 Mercian
from 2005 to 2012, and
is now a keen amateur
photographer

For those that can't

The Veteran Collective was one of those ideas that just came out of nowhere, like all good ideas. I was trying to give back to the veteran community by organising a meet up and doing what I could. Mental health issues are rampant in the modern society, it's not just the prevue of the military. The spectrum of these issues and their effects are huge, yet despite all of this the help available, or more accurately when it's actually needed, is laughable.

A good friend of mine (Gaz who very kindly has done the foreword) suggested I create a platform for it — and here we are, The Veteran Collective. There are a huge amount of veterans doing things like this, and a much better job of it than me. The total lack of help when it's needed is probably the thing that spurs us on to do something ourselves, and for each other.

We all need to realise there is absolutely no point in sitting around waiting for help that isn't going to come, we have to help each other and by doing so help ourselves.

This book is simply a collection of thoughts, poems and stories in everyone's own words, in all its grammatically incorrect and spelling mistake glory!

Hopefully this book can show any veteran, serving, or anyone that reads it there is hope and help out there — you are not alone.

This is our story, for you.

Daz

One of the airborne
memorials at Ft
Bragg North
Carolina

Author

For Amy and Lilly-Mae

The Airborne Memorial at
the National Arboretum

Acknowledgments

These are the incredible people that have contributed and made this book possible;

Dave Radband, Neville Johnson, Josh from Ace of Iron Apparel, Rob 'Smash' Creighton, Lee Davies, DevSoc

I can't thank you all enough, you gave your help, words and encouragement without hesitation - this is what brotherhood means.

My good friend Gaz, it takes a lot to write what he has for the foreword, which is what this is all about. If a WO2 from Hereford can speak out, anyone can - we are not superhuman.

The foreword, midword and lastword

WO 'Gaz'
17 year veteran of the SAS

It was 2017 and I'd been out of the army for 5 years. It was getting late. I was tired. We were arguing again. We never used to argue – when I was 'in'. Now, we seemed to argue a lot. I can't remember what it was about, or 99% of what was said. I can't even remember the question. But I'll never forget my screamed answer.

"Because if I had a gun right now, I would shoot myself in the fucking head"

In 2012 I was forced to leave. Time served. I was a WO2 and had been in the SAS for 17 years. I was 42 years old, fitter than 95% of soldiers, and still had lots to offer. Now, after a slow emotional decline over 5 years, I had hit rock bottom. Once those words were spoken, I couldn't take them back. To utter them wasn't a conscious decision, I had no control. They just came out from somewhere deep inside. I hadn't realised that I had been grieving. Unfortunately, I had grieved many times before, for lives lost too soon. Unfortunately, that came with the job and was almost expected. What I didn't expect, was to have to grieve for the loss of my own life. That was a bit of a shock.

I'd spent the last 5 years being scared and angry. Scared about how I was going to provide for my family. Scared that I didn't know who I was, now I wasn't a soldier. Angry at The Regiment for scrapping me. Angry at The Regiment for not helping. Angry at civvies for not being soldiers. I was even angry that I was scared and scared that I was angry. The problem wasn't being scared and angry, the problem was that I knew what was wrong but didn't want to admit it or confront it.

I'd overcome adversity many times before. These were mostly physical challenges that required a degree of mental toughness. I was comfortable with this. So comfortable, that I would often put myself in challenging situations, just to be challenged. But this was different, this was purely a mental obstacle, something I hadn't experienced. But now those words were out, I had a choice – to listen or not listen, to take action or not take action. I'd never failed at anything. I wasn't going to start now.

I started my journey to recovery. I always knew what I needed to do – think differently and make different choices. When you think about it, life is just a series of choices that we make, based on the values and beliefs that we hold. If we want different choices to the ones that we currently have, we have to change what we value and what we believe. How can we expect others to love us if we don't love ourselves? How can we be accepted if we are not accepting? How can we be understood, if we don't understand? I stopped dwelling on the past. I stopped waiting for the help that was never coming. If I was going to escape the feeling of being isolated on my own island, in the middle of a vast emotional ocean, that I myself had created in my own mind. I was going to have to do it myself. The chopper wasn't coming. It was time to act.

I started to build my lifeboat, one positive thought at a time. I wrote 2 lists. What made me feel good and what didn't. I got rid of everything that detracted from my self-worth and did more of what empowered me. Now when a negative thought appears, I change it for a positive one. It's my choice what I think about. It always has been, I just didn't realise it.

I now feel different to what I did. I remember years ago I was on a boat with a few other blokes and we capsized as we approached the beach. The surf was pretty rough, and the current was strong. I had a life preserver on but didn't want to be the first to pop it. The ridicule would have been too much – better to drown that to look a knob! I remember being a couple of feet away from my mate and not being able to reach him, he was struggling too. Although we couldn't help each other physically, when our eyes met, we connected, we both knew that even though we were fighting our own battles, we were rooting for each other. That gave me strength. The strength to swim to shore, the strength to survive (without popping my life preserver and looking weak).

If you are reading this book you are on the same journey has its contributors. It is a journey that you have to make yourself, others can't do it for you. But gain strength from the knowledge that we are all rooting for you. Just remember, anytime you feel lonely – you are not alone.

Gaz

Stranger To Myself

What have I become
A stranger too many
A stranger to myself
Looking in the mirror
I see him staring at me
I can't find me in there
I don't recognise him
How long have you been here?
Completely unknown to myself
Engulfed in numbness to all
Who is this old man I see?
Grey hair wrinkled face
I see rage in his eyes
Anger in his soul
Do I know you?
Looking through me
Starring at nothing
Who have I become
What have I become?
A stranger to all

Neville Johnson

Sometimes The Places Closest To Home,

are the furthest away.

Darren Roberts

Sometimes the places closest to home,

are the furthest away

I couldn't wait to get out. Having spent my entire childhood wanting to be nothing but a soldier, once my time was up all I wanted to do was leave. The boredom, monotony, all wrapped up in what seemed like an endless stream of utterly pointless tasks. When you're in your 20's you've got all the answers and no questions - having joined at 16 and left at 25, I felt like I'd lived a lifetime already.

It's only now many years later that I appreciate my 9 years of service for what it actually was, and what it actually gave me. I wouldn't be the person I am today and I wouldn't be doing what I am today, if it wasn't for the fact I had served - that's including all the utterly pointless bullshit we had to do. Learning to embrace my military past in a positive way is also learning to embrace myself, having spent so many years trying to ignore it.

In a feckless civilian society where there seems to be no social norm or sense of values, and no one seems to care about anything anymore - what was the point in me caring? If they don't care what I've done, why, where and who with - why should I? That's the trick though isn't it? It's not actually about 'them', there is no 'us' or 'them' this is about 'all of us'. We all left service for many different reasons, but that doesn't diminish or take away anything that we achieved or the things that we ought to be proud of. However expecting a civilian society to either know or care about that is at best naive, at worst it is completely stupid.

You may have been in a firefight in Afghan, patrolled West Belfast or South Armagh back in the day - but you could've also been a single parent struggling to make ends meet whilst living in squalor.

We've all had struggles in our own way, we've all had battles to fight - not all of them involves incoming rounds and not all exclusively the domain of the military. Civvies have shit going on as well, as do first responders.

One thing you did in the military, was a lot of travelling. Leaving as a 25 year old having served 9 years, I'd already been from one side of the world to the other. From Arctic Canada, Central America, to the South Atlantic and Europe. No matter how far we travelled, it was close to home that was the strangest. Whether it was Brecon, Catterick Training Area, Salisbury Plain or STANTA - looking at the distant glow of a town lights at night, with people going about their lives whilst I froze to death in a shell scrape felt so distant.

Northern Ireland was even more bizarre. Coming from the North of England, it could've been Leeds or Manchester - there's a WH Smiths except I'm in full rig, with a weapon and live rounds. As I was the crow on the fire team was also top cover, again making the experience even more surreal as it looked like driving around home.

Every time I did return home, I felt a little more detached from friends and family. They were as unaware of what was happening 200 miles away as 2,000 miles away. Each deployment meant being closer to your team mates (whether you were friends or not), and I went home less and less. The need to be around people that spoke the same language as me, same brutal no mercy sense of humour. The longer I was in the more foreign home became. We spend significant amounts of time on Pre-Deployment training, comprehensive and intense training packages to hone all TTP's. This ensures everyone is on their 'A' game for the job and last for several weeks.

When it came to leaving the service, I had 1 day of handing kit back in, walking around camp to get a signature from various elements to say I'd handed in what I needed and/or nothing else was needed. The final signature was in the camp HQ building to hand my ID card in, get the signature - and that was it. I don't think the clerk even said anything. Leaving the camp gates that afternoon I was now a civilian - my unit was away so there were no goodbyes.

Looking back now, it's an utterly fucking ridiculous way to discharge someone into a life they've never lived. Especially if, like me, they think they're going to piss civilian life because how hard can it be? I'm not hard targeting anywhere so happy and easy days - winning. You then find yourself surrounded by the fuckery of the disorganised jack as fuck zero accountable civilian world. Where no one does what they say they're going to do, when they said they'd do it or care that they didn't

Now you're actually home,

you've never been so far away

One of the many stunning churches in Normandy France, many still bearing the scars of the ferocious fighting.

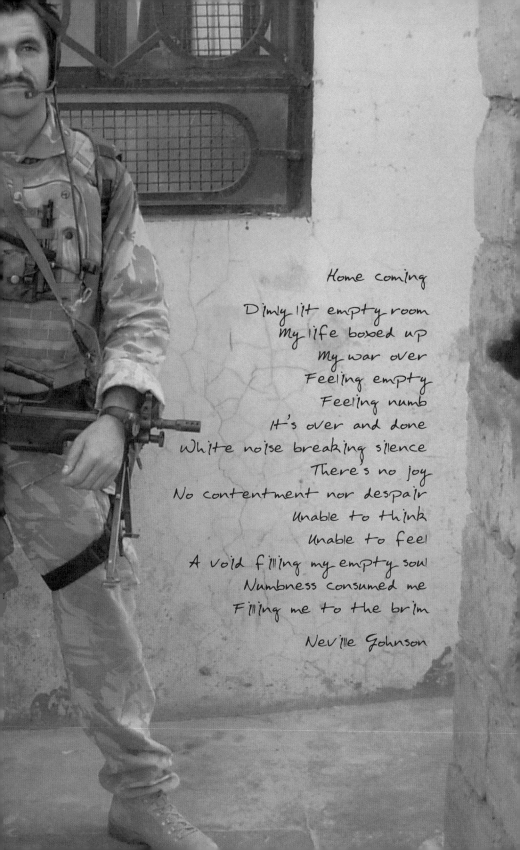

Home coming

Dimly lit empty room
My life boxed up
My war over
Feeling empty
Feeling numb
It's over and done
White noise breaking silence
There's no joy
No contentment nor despair
Unable to think
Unable to feel
A void filling my empty soul
Numbness consumed me
Filling me to the brim

Neville Johnson

Author

Sub Arctic Canada, 90's

Darren Roberts

Civilian life is the most extreme environment
you will ever operate in.

It took 2 years of training, to the point where the picture on the frozen lake was taken, just below the Arctic Circle.

Extreme environments are the proving grounds of professional soldiering, whether that's the jungle, snow or desert. The saying, 'do the basics well' takes on it's true meaning in these conditions. When the ambient temp is -32°, most of what you do is about looking after yourself and your kit. Nothing can be left to chance or half arsed as it could cost you (and your team mates) anything up to and including your life. Just as it is in the jungle or desert - and in combat, which is what you're training for.

The most extreme environment by far, civvie street - the one theatre of operations I had precisely fuck all training in. At first it's like being on leave, then it's not - in any way. You're not returning to camp, you're here now mate, this is you and it's what you wanted. Fuck.

I wish I'd reached out years ago, to help with transition stress which leads to anxiety and depression - all expertly hidden of course. It can't be hidden forever, even if it takes 5, 10 or 15 years to come out.

Don't be ashamed of not knowing how to deal with the
thing you've never been trained for.

Newfoundland, mid 90's

Without realising I have subconsciously
gone away
Pushed people away from me away from
it all
Gradually creating the void between me
and the world
Digging away at my trench more each
day and night
Escaping deeper with every inch I
orchestrated
Distance myself further from humanity
My inner voice begging to stop
Deep in me in my depth of what I
have become
I accept it all
I acknowledge it is me
For I don't blame them nor you
I chose this desolate existence

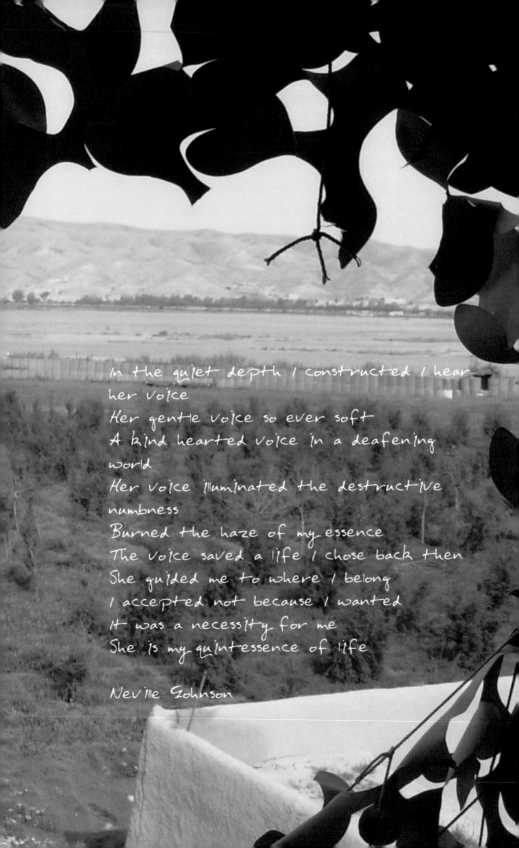

In the quiet depth I constructed I hear her voice
Her gentle voice so ever soft
A kind hearted voice in a deafening world
Her voice illuminated the destructive numbness
Burned the haze of my essence
The voice saved a life I chose back then
She guided me to where I belong
I accepted not because I wanted
It was a necessity for me
She is my quintessence of life

Neville Johnson

Dave Radband

Peace in war

I miss it because it was the most real thing I've had. There's no bull shit. There's no grey. There's no maybe or might be. There's no questioning. There's fight and no fight. Life and death. Brothers and enemy. Glory and death. Simple.

We have missions. But our main mission, to fight, and keep our brothers alive. You love the man next to you. Even the ones I didn't particularly like, I love. I love every last one of them. They are the reason I miss war. In war, we didn't have bills, jobs, and families dividing our time. It was just us, brothers. We literally saw the best and the worst times of our lives together. We would spend every minute fearing, fighting, miserable, happy, all together, as one brotherhood. We didn't have anything but our weapons and our brothers.

I also had a reason in life. It wasn't grey, or questionable in the way of wondering what it should be. I knew what my life was, and what I was meant for. I am a warrior. I'm a war fighter. It's why I'm here. I face my enemy. I don't hide. I fight or I die. We would talk about Valhalla and how the only death for a warrior that is respectful and beautiful, was death in battle. We believe in Valhalla, it made us fearless. It made us think about how we are so similar to other warriors and how war, no matter what century or what side you are on, bonds all warriors. And of course, my war was vastly different from the Vikings or even the world wars, but it was still war. We still lost brothers and it has scarred us for life.

Such raw emotion and pure adrenaline. Living in fear becomes so addictive. As much as it fucked with me, and made me edgy, and gave me some serious anxiety afterwards, it made me feel the most alive I've ever felt.

I miss the firefights, door kicking and assaults. The all out war. I loved that feeling of a good fire fight. There were many fights where we had air support come in quickly and it ended. Or you were ambushed so fast, and effectively you couldn't fight back right away, they where shit fights.   But the fights that were toe-to-toe, loved.

I loved that adrenaline.

        I miss that feeling of knowing I could die.

Memories of the Valley

I can write just pour me a glass
            Words flow and fall
I can write just pour me more
Thoughts and feelings return
        My memories of war
A distant life I live no more
Memories pouring flooding in
I need to write pour me more
    A time, a place forgotten
I need to write to remember
            Pour some more

Neville Johnson

Unknown location, mid 90's

Clearly it's somewhere supposed to be temperate,
as I'm in jungle boots, so obviously the weather
is dogshit whilst in a shell scrape getting our
'sugar cookie' on.

Darren Roberts

Get comfortable with

being uncomfortable?

Whilst I understand the sentiment, it literally makes no sense. It's the usual soundbite word salad bullshit which is awash on the intellectual BDSM dungeon that is social media. I much prefer 'there is no growth in comfort', that at least makes some sense.

As a soldier in any teeth arm unit, you're going to be 'uncomfortable' a lot - physically, mentally and emotionally. Being told to ignore it and essentially 'man up' is a mistake. This is more than simply 'embracing the suck', it's a directed and conscious effort to allow the discomfort into your body and mind. This can be in a 12 hour ambush in the jungle, lying there soaking wet through with all the lovely creatures nature has to offer crawling on you. The survival shelter in -30 artic Canada, or the dreaded mind numbing time dilation of stagging on. It can also be the anxiety of how that household bill is going to be paid, will you be stuck where you are in life and missing the camaraderie of your team mates.

Don't get comfortable being uncomfortable - no good came of ignoring anything. Embrace where and what you are, as this can help you move forward.

Then maybe, just maybe, you don't need to move as far

as you think

Sat on a C130 in USA waiting to jump, using US
equipment, sweating our tits off as it's about
elventy zillion degrees inside the aircraft.

Author

Life we take for granted
So many things we take for granted
Sitting here reminiscing
Contemplating my life
Thinking and daydreaming
Thoughts about returning home
Lost track of the days
Days with no names attached
The unforgiving Helmand heat
Sweat exuding through my pores
I can hear the Sangin sound
Talking to me filling my mind

These quiet moments breaking me The
feeling difficult to describe Feeling
tense feeling tight Unable to relax
God I hate this feeling in me These
quite moments breaking me Breaking
me bit by bit Waiting for
something to happen Reminiscing
contemplating Daydreaming and
thinking These quiet moments
Breaking me more and more.

Neville Johnson

Sword Beach, Normandy, France 7th June 2019

Josh

Ace Of Iron Apparel

Why do we miss it?

That's a question that plagues the mind of those who have seen war. Why would we miss something so dangerous, so harrowing, and so emotional? However the same question can be reversed to understand why we do indeed miss war. Why would you not miss something so exciting, so liberating, so testing, and so exhilarating?

In an uncanny way, war provides a sense of freedom. It provides you with an ability to cast aside worries back home. It provides a sense of liberation to truly live each day as it comes, to focus only on the task at hand. People preach about living in the moment all over social media, but only few of us have and will ever experience that true sense of freedom. We miss war because it was the pinnacle of brotherhood, nothing could break that bond that we few have shared in war. There's no shame in admitting that.

"A just war is better than an unjust peace"
Unknown Stoic.

Fighting for a just cause will always favour an unjust peace in the warriors eye. Fighting for something provides a sense of purpose. This can be applied to all walks of life and not just that of a wartime environment. For anything in life that is worth fighting for will provide the greater reward, no matter how big or small that may be.
Most of us left a piece behind after experiencing war. We were not the same person before than we were after. Although this is commonly misinterpreted as a curse, it is often a blessing. That

person you were before has lived their life, so take the lessons learnt from that past and bring it to your present.

Acknowledge the short comings and push forward, suppress the enemy, and win the firefight.

You know the drill.

OUT!

Bosnia/Serbia Border , mid 90's

If you can't practice your catalogue poses in AO's, are you even soldiering? I've been friends with lad on the right since we were kids, he was my team commander.

Dave Radband
Remembrance Day 2016

I had been out of the military for almost 2 years. I went to the Local parade as a civilian, with my medals pinned to my chest. In the silence, a bugle sounded The Last Post. And in that moment, suddenly the memories of my time at war came flooding back.

Something inside had snapped. Something had me by the balls. I was panicking standing there in the ceremony - emotional. That sound of the bugle reminded me of the moment it was announced every time a brother was lost.

Friends, killed or injured, flashed in front of my eyes: My Afghan soldiers, my brothers Kev, Dale, Kyle, Steve, John, Multiple Welsh guards id seen torn up.

For five years I had been suppressing these thoughts.

I thought I was fine but all of a sudden I wasn't any more. That door I kept shut, had just been blown off the hinges. This is how PTSD is, it's something that creeps up on you. And I didn't see it coming.

Once you've been shot at it never leaves your mind. The rounds that come near you sound like a crack of a whip. There were countless operations where I was in a near-death situations, I've been blown up in armoured vehicles, I've had my equipment on my person hit by enemy bullets. I wasn't hurt myself, but many were.

When you have adrenaline pumped into you every single day for months, when you come home that's missing. Time moves slow. People moved slowly. It was so quiet. I needed to find my fix.

That's when my troubles
                                        REALLY started.

Dave

Josh Ace of Iron

Accept yourself?

2 years ago I was fully diagnosed with PTSD and BPD (borderline personality disorder). See, you can have more than one mental illness at the same time, or one mental illness can trigger other illnesses. So for me, I'm living with two mental illnesses. From when I was a young child until I was a teenager, I was mentally and emotionally effected by a few events. One of them being bullied all through school.

It took years to get properly diagnosed. I will be brutally honest with you, the path to recovery isn't easy. For a long time, it feels like the bad days outweigh the good days and it feels like it's a never-ending journey. This was why therapy was so important for me. I knew if I quit I would end up on a destructive path that will end up with me in prison or worse dead.

But the hardest thing for me to accept was that this is something that will be a part of me for the rest of my life. Because I knew so little about mental illnesses, I just assumed that after a few months of therapy and swallowing pills it would get better and go away. But that's not true. For me, my illnesses will always be apart of me. I'v slowly learnt to cope. I'm learnt to survive.

I wasn't going to let my mental illnesses beat me. I've said in posts before, *I WILL NEVER QUIT!!* It's like learning to tame a lion-I eventually backed it into submission. And while it will always follow me around, I can't spend the rest of my life wondering and waiting for a relapse to happen again. Instead, I just do the work. I use some of the strategies I have learned in therapy to help cope, and I simply just live. I still suffer from my disorders and I still have to work to manage them. But now, when all starts feeling lost again, I don't ignore the warning signs. I take precautionary measures like seeking support and health care, pouring myself into something that makes me happy, practicing self-care, and most of all, loving myself.

If or when I do relapse again, I am prepared for battle

    I am ready to fight

Dave

A piece of me I gave away
A piece of you I took away
Some of me died that day
Neville Johnson

Josh

Ace Of Iron Apparel

The loss of a fellow royal marine this weekend sparked a lot of thought. Life is a war-zone, some days are of great importance, some are not. Some days are filled with emotions that can be completely flipped in the blink on an eye. You may go from a feeling of immense victory and pride, to having your soul ripped away in the next moment. War is a place where a little bit of brass can impact the lives of not just everybody on that Op, but those back home, the families, the friends, the loved ones - the effect is relentless.

It is however strangely peaceful to live in times of war, where there are no distractions other than the task at hand, and coming back to reality is often more difficult than anything experienced on the battlefield. Where the guy behind the till at the supermarket doesn't give a shit about the ambush you were in 24 hours ago, although you must realise those who have never experienced war cannot comprehend that reality, it is not their fault, we chose to live that life, and what a fucking great life it was.

It is important however to realise that you are surrounded by brothers who would give their lives to save yours, both on and off the field of battle. You are never out of the fight, you are never truly defeated, not when you have people to your left and right. Taking care of the mind is as important as taking care of the body.

I'll leave this with one word.

Talk.

SUR CETTE PLAGE DE
SAINT-AUBIN, A L'AUBE
DU 6 JUIN 1944, A 7ʰ30
FUT ETABLIE UNE TÊTE
DE PONT PAR LE RÉGIMENT
D'INFANTERIE CANADIENNE
DES "NORTH SHORE",
OUVRANT LA VOIE AU
48 ᵉᵐᵉ COMMANDO
DES "ROYAL MARINES"

Juno Beach, Normandy, France 6th June 2019

Darren Roberts

Loneliness is seen as such a sad thing,

but there can be beauty in solace.

Being on your own is often viewed as a negative thing, however time with yourself to be yourself doesn't have to be sad. If the environment is negative, sad and 'lonely' then that's what you'll feel, consider your environment.

Being on Juno Beach absorbing that 75 years ago to the day, the very place was awash with the horrors of war - was more about connecting with the humanity of the sacrifice than the sadness. In what was one of the last conflicts to involve sovereignty rather than oil driven geopolitics by a corrupt political class - the sense of duty humbling, the sacrifice staggering.

In a world where nothing means anything anymore unless it's insta swipe right hacked 6K HD reality tv which isn't reality - to be somewhere alone with thoughts, appreciate the sacrifice and reflect on paths chosen and choices yet made. It gave me true context, guide my thoughts without the tsunami of consumerism white noise. A place where its history can flow through you like a river, washing away the bullshit to give clarity to your mind and purpose.

A jet wash for the soul to strip away the layers,
leaving the real you to move forward.

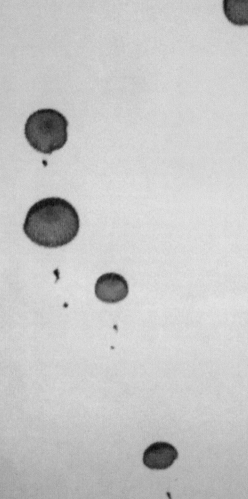

PX4 Jump, unknown DZ, mid 90's Author

Darren Roberts

Partners in crime, soulmates,
best friends.

We've been married for 16 years, and together for 18 years. With the highest of highs, along with lows so deep and dark they felt like black holes where nothing but gravity escapes - but only to pull you in further.

Up until 6 years ago, I never spoke of my military background, what I did or why - including to my wife. Not because of some chilling PTSDesque reason, just simply that I was completely 'away motivated' from it. Then slowly but surely I began to embrace, or reconnect is probably a better way to put it, my military self 5 years ago.

I loved introducing her to basic weapons training and the range. She thrived on the weapons handling and marksmanship (under my shite instruction) with the Glock and M4. The power dynamics are complex in any relationship, however for once she listened to any instruction or direction I gave without any arguments. For a complete novice, she was brilliant! It was something from my past I was able to bring into the 'now' of our relationship - in a positive way.

There are things which fundamentally make us who we are, some nice - some not.

If you've hidden them all in the past maybe,
they don't all belong there?

Combat veterans

Our darker residue of our previous lives
stored away
Keeping the darkness at bay
In quiet moments we hear past
conversations and jokes
Stories being told with a dark sense of
humour
Father and son
Combat veterans

Neville Johnson

Ranville Cemetery, Normandy, France 8th June 2019

Darren Roberts

We all experience loss in some way.

I hadn't really ever accepted the loss of anyone. The circumstances are usually so sudden, having only spoken or been with them days, hours or minutes before - it's impossible to accept they're truly gone. Somewhere, somehow, I convinced myself they're still alive. I can pick the conversation up with someone where we left it 10 years before, so it's not a stretch to the imagination to maintain the illusion they're still around. Then years later when you least expect it, you might be confronted with this loss and what it truly means.

Loss doesn't have to be 'someone', it can also be a 'something', like the life you had with the friends you became a man with in service. We all wanted to leave the service for our various reasons, and that can mask 'the loss' we should feel. We should recognise that, loss - the loss of everything we've known. Maybe even mourn or grieve that loss, to really move on by accepting it for what it was.

I know my friends are dead, as cliché as it sounds they live on in my memories, which is not the same as pretending they're still alive. I also now embrace my military service, rather than run away pretending it didn't happen.

This doesn't ignore the utter bullshit we did or saw,
        but we can make peace with it and celebrate what was good,
                whilst remembering those friends.

PEGASUS
BRIDGE

The British 6th Airborne Division landed near this bridge
on the night of 5th June 1944, as a spearhead to the
Allied Armies of Liberation.

La 6ème Division Aéroportée Britannique a atterri à proximité
de ce pont dans la nuit du 5 Juin 1944, en tant que flèche
des Armées Alliées de Libération.

Darren Roberts

The honour of service, the tragedy of sacrifice

To serve your country, the flag, defend your homeland from aggressors and oppressors. The nobility of it, honour with selfless distinction. The idea of a citizen soldier stretches back to 500bc and the mythical Spartans, an austere life spent in service. The ruling class did not shy away from the realities, responsibilities or consequences of war by serving themselves, including their own sons and daughters right up to WW2. Our own Prince William & Harry serving to the best of their abilities, despite the constraints places on them. After 20 years of conflict on the middle east, we are seeing former serving soldiers appearing as elected officials.

I wanted to be 'more than myself', to be a part of something that made a difference in a world crippled with indifference. Maybe I was born in the wrong century. I'd wanted to serve since I was 4 years old, counting the days until I was 16 and able to join.

Do not mistake my patriotism for racism
My service for ignorance
Or my pride as blindness
Do not mistake my silence as being complicit
My calmness for acceptance
Or my kindness for weakness
                    Anon

We are where we are because of those that went before us, they paid with their lives in a different time and different world. Remembering is not celebrating, it is humility and memory.
If we let it become history, we won't remember and if we don't remember

we cannot break the cycle.

ALL
WHO
SERVED
RESPECT
THANK YOU
FOR OUR
TODAY.
IN
REMEMBRANCE

Ranville Cemetery, Normandy, June 7th 2019

Sangin Nights

3am conversations
High on coffee
Low on life
Lucid dreaming
Magic wonder
Sangin nights
Seeing green
All can be seen
In the valley
Deafening sound of silence

Neville Johnson

Dave Radband

The first time I tried to kill myself, I thought I was doing what was in everyone's best interest. I wholeheartedly believed it was what the people in my life wanted. I felt that I was nothing but a burden, a nuisance and a catalyst for pain for anyone who had the misfortune of coming into contact with me. But more importantly, I tried to end my life because the person I saw when I looked at myself in the mirror, wasn't the person I had been looking at for 30 years.

My parents found me! Hanging in the loft space, unconscious. They managed to revive me and I woke up in my mother's arms. "Are you kidding me – it didn't work? Shit, now what?". I closed my eyes, hoping I'd pass out and not come to again. It was then I started to cry my eyes out. The energy that I had in being so angry that I was not dead is the kind of energy we need to stay alive.

We should tell each other we love each other and that we care for each other, rather than just assuming that everyone knows how we feel about them. We should also rely on each other more for emotional support and encouragement.

If you're having any suicidal thoughts at all, it's serious. I urge you to reach out to people close to you, no matter how much it feels like you can't. Please don't fall into the same mind trap I did. You matter. You are valued and important, regardless of how much your demons tell you otherwise. If you are hurting the way I still do sometimes, you are in my thoughts and I want you to hold on.

People often tell me that I seem like someone who is meant to do great things. I've thought of that often, wondering whether they genuinely meant it, or if its just a platitude meant to cheer up a depressed man. What I do know for sure is that the only way I'll ever find out is if I continue to live.

So let's make a promise, you and I, that we will fight and we will survive. We are stronger than we give ourselves credit for, and we are stronger than our demons. We've got this.

In the UK, Samaritans can be contacted on 116 123 or email jo@samaritans.org. In the US, the National Suicide Prevention Lifeline is 1-800-273-8255.

Waiting listing watching
Observing looking and scanning
Checking arcs ears pinned back
Waiting knowing its coming
Ready finger on the trigger
Deafening sound of Sangin town
Heart beating pounding hard
RPG breaking the silence
Returning fire
Tracers lighting the dawn
Sangin valley greeting the day

Neville Johnson

Dave Radband

You get out of the military and your whole life spreads before you. Wide open. You don't know what you want to do, and you don't know what you should be doing. There's no one now to define what the shape of your days and nights looks like. And no threat to your existence that makes the future seem irrelevant.

You're stranded out here with no clue what to do in this civilian world. You don't want to be a civilian (you'll never be one of them, don't worry), but you DO have to live among them and find some way to make a life.

No, you can't go back, but you don't know how to go forward because all you long for is what you left behind. Every civilian you know assumes you're relieved and happy to be done with the military. They don't stop to think that you're like a pro athlete who, at the height of his career, gets injured and will never play again. You don't just face career choices, you face a void of purpose. It's not that you just lost your job, it's that you lost your whole identity. But even more important, you lost something very few people will EVER experience: What it is to be fully, deeply alive.

This isn't about finding the right job or career path and hoping it will fulfil you. This is about the "who you are" side of purpose. And it's spiritual, because you are an eternal spirit having an earthly experience. Until you solve the "who you are" side, nothing you do will feel like purpose.

Even if you can't prevent problems from occurring, good situational awareness will provide you with a sense of control, a sense of awareness and calmness that will allow you to overcome any setbacks quickly and keep pushing forward. If you combine your knowledge of situational awareness with emotional intelligence (controlled aggression), you will develop a cool, calm and focused mindset willing and able to react in a positive manner to the environment around you.

Build mental resilience by doing something different.

From random tasks to unanticipated attacks, a soldiers mindset is all about preparing for the unknown. In our language, this is called 'Situational Awareness'.

In essence, it is the ability of your mind to pay attention to what's going or happening around you. Of course, a military environment will require entirely different levels of tactics and mental conditioning techniques to develop this tactical ability but you too can practice this technique at any point and time in life.

How do we do it in the military? Mental conditioning drills in the military are reinforced by positive thinking, controlled aggressive thoughts, relaxation and defusing of destructive emotions. The training involves thinking of new situations and circumstances that might (or might not) happen in the future.

How can you do it? Start by giving your brain new situations and simulations on a daily level. Routine is the recipe to safety (comfort zone) and to develop mental courage, you'll have to break the patterns of routine.

Start going out to new places. Make a point to meet new people. Try saying yes to new experiences and activities. Pick up a new hobby or a useful skill. To be successful, you must learn how to build the right amount of mental confidence and preparedness and for that you must embrace the unknown. Have the courage to try out something new and different whenever life gives you an opportunity.

Yes, you might fail, be shit at it or make a complete fool of yourself.

So what? At least, you'll be wiser,

                                      fuller and better prepared

    than anyone who doesn't even want to face their fears.

C'EST ICI MÊME QUE, LE 6 JUIN 1944
A 0 HEURE 16 A ATTERRI LE PLANEUR HORSA
DU COMMANDANT R. J. HOWARD,
DE L'OXFORDSHIRE AND BUCKINGHAMSHIRE
LIGHT INFANTRY, COMMANDANT L'OPERATION
DESTINEE A ASSURER LE PRISE DU PONT.
SE TROUVAIENT A BORD AVEC LUI LES
PILOTES SERGENTS — CHEF WALLWORK
ET AINSWORTH LE LIEUTENANT
H. D. BROTHERIDGE ET 28 SOLDATS.

THE HORSA GLIDER OF MAJOR R. J. HOWARD,
OXFORDSHIRE AND BUCKINGHAMSHIRE LIGHT
INFANTRY, WHO COMMANDED THE OPERATION
TO CAPTURE THE BRIDGE LANDED ON THIS
SPOT TOGETHER WITH LIEUTENANT
H. D. BROTHERIDGE AND 28 SOLDIERS. AT
0016 HOURS ON 6 JUNE 1944 THE PILOTS
WERE STAFF SERGEANTS
WALLWORK AND AINSWORTH

Dave Radband

Depression is a freakin' monster, a beast. If you haven't experienced suicidal thoughts before, then you can't speak to the heaviness, the solidness, the loneliness, and the shame that exists parallel to depression. It's exhausting!   The terrible reality and truth of depression is that sometimes all the help isn't enough.

One of the pernicious parts of depression is that it tells you that you aren't worthy of receiving help, of succeeding, of living; in other words, you think you aren't worthy of doing the very thing you need to do to hopefully save your life. So then what?

If you're concerned about someone, pick up the phone and tell them. Don't know what to say? Tell them that, too. Often it's not what you say but the fact that you said something at all that can make someone feel like they are connected to something larger than themselves. Often after someone dies by suicide, their loved ones will say they had no idea or didn't see any signs the person was depressed. Mental illness is tricky in that it knows how to cover itself up when others are around.

So don't wait! There's nothing wrong with telling someone you LOVE that they MATTER to you and its important to you that they're in your life. If they aren't depressed, they'll be touched by the gesture. But if they are, you may have just saved their life. Brothers, if I see you hurting, I will acknowledge your pain. If I see you slipping, I will say something. If I see you buried under the weight of depression - unable to reach out for help - I will reach out to you.

If I see you are drowning,

I will throw you a line.

Dave

Quiet times

During the quiet times
My mind wonder
Thoughts drift
For a moment it felt real
It felt like home
I was home
For now I'm here in the valley
I'm up I'm moving
Running for cover
Sangin my wonderful wild

Neville Johnson

Dave Radband

Dealing with Mental health can be an everyday struggle. It's definitely true that some days are worse than others, but I've learned to manage it, to become aware of my symptoms, my triggers, and to remain in control.

However, this has not always been the case. It's only this year that I have come to understand what's going on inside the relationship between my body and mind. Awareness is the key to prevention and that is why I like to share with you my story's of battling PTSD and BPD. I don't want anyone else to feel the way I have done, to feel trapped and isolated by mental health problems and to not be able to see a light at the end of the tunnel.

I would spend days on end in bed, unwilling, or even unable to move, for mental health can be so debilitating that it becomes physically disabling. I would hardly eat or drink, refuse to socialise, want to escape but not be able to as there was nowhere for me to go, knowing that I would always have to return to my room at the end of the day. It's a vicious cycle that, without help, is almost impossible to break.

The first big step for me was accepting, or as is often more difficult, realising that I was mentally unwell (after 2 very close suicide attempts). It took me a long time to do this. The days I spent lying in my bedroom, telling myself I was 'just bored', was me refusing to accept the reality that was my mental ill health.

I've seen a huge improvement in my mental health and I am a completely different person as a result. My mental health is still there, I think it always will be, but I can manage it to the extent that it doesn't affect my ability to function in day-to-day life. There are so many other people just like me who struggle with depression and that is why it is so important to raise awareness in order to prevent others from reaching the same horrible depths that I did.

I want to help create a world with good mental health for all and I hope my instagram has been helpful, or even inspiring this year.

Josh Ace of Iron

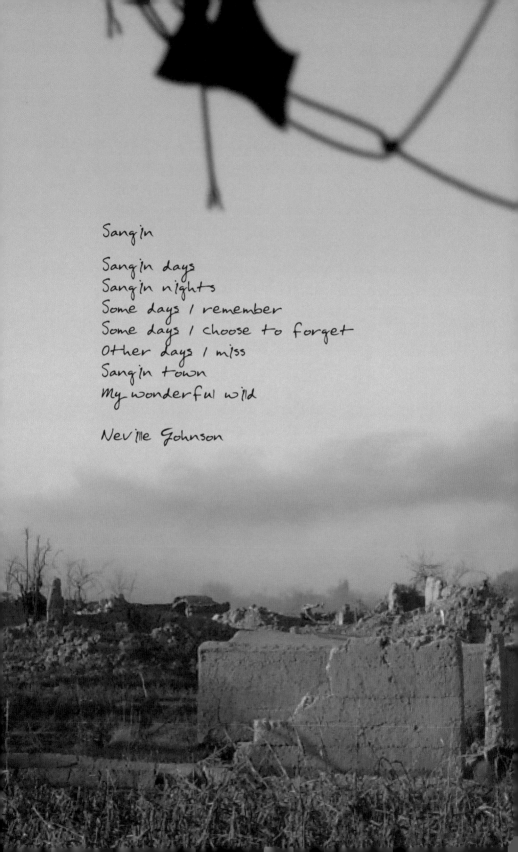

Sangin

Sangin days
Sangin nights
Some days I remember
Some days I choose to forget
Other days I miss
Sangin town
My wonderful wild

Neville Johnson

Dave Radband

There are words that no soldier ever wants to hear, but I've had to shout them into my radio.,"Contact IED! Wait out!"

We had been briefed earlier that there was approximately 20 IEDs in the area. I had an eerie feeling about the surroundings. There was something spooky about them, it made the hairs on the back of my neck stand up. My teams mission that day was to clear a series of compounds, but as we entered one of them we where contacted with PKM fire. I pushed forward to check for ground sign, IEDs within the compound. I had nothing to do this with, just my eyes. After deciding it was safe, we pushed in for cover and held the compound.

We pushed onto the target compounds. As we did so I was hit by a wave of sound and debris, it seemed to be moving in slow motion; I got launched off my feet and landed on my back. Initially I thought it was me that had stood on the device. I shit myself!! I gave myself a quick check over and realised I was not in any pain apart from my face and head. I had taken a big blow to my helmet, that also saved my life.

I sent the initial contact report over my radio. "Contact IED. Wait out." Through the thick dust, I saw my Afghan interpreter lying in the alleyway. Both of his legs were missing, his left arm was also missing. I called for a medic and then started giving my initial first aid. Sadly he died while I was working on him. The Taliban had not gone away. The crack of bullets split the air as a PKM position tried to take more of us, they had clearly heard the IED blast. I got the rest of my team together, by this time I had a support element with me from 1 Welsh guards.

I periodically remind myself of my brothers that never made it back. Every day brought a very real danger of stepping on or driving over an IED, engaging in deadly firefights with a determined enemy, or not making it into cover before incoming rockets and mortars exploded.

Our unit had lost a lot of guys in 2009. To this day, it doesn't get any easier for me to think about it,

but these life experiences have shown me a brighter more positive life

Dave

Author

Ready for a jump using US equipment.

Rob Creighton

F u c k   M o t i v a t i o n

Fuck Motivation; Ignore it, look beyond it, reach past it and step over it. Punch it in the fucking face if you have to....it is not your ally, it doesn't have allies.

Motivation opposes you, it uses you and thinks of itself as better than anyone and anything. It's only intention is to steal your energy from where it should be focussed and distract you from achieving your Everest.

Motivation is a toxic drug; the more you use it the more it consumes you. It takes from you and doesn't ever give back. Each time you get high with it, the less of a high it provides.

Fuck motivation; Fuck the influencers and the charlatans. Fuck photoshop, and it's lies. Fuck chemically enhanced bodies. Fuck the liars, plagiarisers & fraudsters. Fuck the smoke & mirrors.

FUCK MOTIVATION

Josh

Ace Of Iron Apparel

Once a man sees war,

the world will always look a little different.

You'll notice that a post-tour cheeseburger tastes like nothing you can imagine.

You'll notice that life is trivial, that it can be taken away in a heart beat, but in that same moment can be saved and given back.

You'll notice the value in every moment, how in one minute a brother was stood by your side, and how they slipped away the next.

You'll notice that you should have called your parents more, because even those trivial chats about the weather are often the nicest part of the day.

You'll notice the strange limboing emptiness you feel when you hear the sound of a helicopter, a strange conflict of knowing your either en-route home, or en-route to fight.

You'll notice how little you are valued by the rest of the world, but to a select few, you will notice you are the most valuable person on the planet.

You'll notice the solace of a warm summers day, or the fresh air of a crisp winters morning, and savour every second. You'll notice how horrific the world can be.

You'll notice those brothers you can no longer share words or a beer with, then you'll notice that feeling of anger and despair.

You'll notice that life seems to be moving on, and you'll notice the guilt. But what you must really try to notice, is that feeling of elation when you rediscover your sense of purpose, your focus, your drive, your desire to succeed.
Then, when the smoke clears, you'll notice that today, you are a better person that you were yesterday, and that the world, no matter how horrific, can be a beautiful place after all.

That is how a man who has seen war notices the world.

All be it a little differently.

Josh

Fear is healthy, panic is deadly

We've all heard it in motivational soundbite jargon - Be Fearless. Don't let fear rule you! Fear is the enemy! Of course, it's total utter fucking bullshit word salad. Emotions are not something you can ignore or think your way out of - but you can certainly work to understand them and if they really are what you think they are. 'Fear' for one person may be 'excitement' to another, and the physical reaction may be almost identical for both.

> "We suffer more often in imagination
> than we do in reality."
> Seneca

How much is real and how much imagined, if you could change the way you 'feel' about a thing or situation does it change the reality of it? Does changing the way you 'feel' about a jump from a C130 using US equipment which you have no confidence in, change the reality? Probably not - therefore those emotions can be used to help not hinder.

"Everyone faces up more bravely to a thing for which he has long prepared himself, sufferings, even being withstood if they have been trained for in advance. Those who are unprepared, on the other hand, are panic-stricken by the most insignificant happenings.

We must see to it that nothing takes us by surprise. And since it is invariably unfamiliarity that makes a thing more formidable than it really is, this habit of continual reflection will ensure

that no form of adversity finds you a complete
                                        beginner."

                                                     Seneca

'Fear' is a physiological reaction to something, by embracing and
understanding it rather than ignoring it - you grasp the reality of it.
Whether that's a jump from a Herc, a firefight, your perception of
what others think of you, or what you should be doing in your new
totally unprepared for civilian life.

"In general remember that it is we who torment, we
who make difficulties for ourselves — that is, our
opinions do."

                                                  Epictetus

Fear is healthy, panic is deadly.

Juno Beach, Normandy, France, 6th June 2019

No more fear
My time came to an end
Mission over mission done
My last footprint left in the Sangin sand
Tired body exhausted soul
Sleeplessness my companion no more
My face and hands caked in dirt
My eyes tells the tale
The Sangin valley tale

I am drained of strength
Some days only but a blur
Gaze into nothing
My thousand yard stare
I am ready here
Take me home
Take me please
                    Neville Johnson

Dealing with Mental health can be an everyday struggle. It's definitely true that some days are worse than others, but I've learned to manage it, to become aware of my symptoms, my triggers, and to remain in control.

However, this has not always been the case. It's only this year that I have come to understand what's going on inside the relationship between my body and mind. Awareness is the key to prevention and that is why I like to share with you my story's of battling PTSD and BPD. I don't want anyone else to feel the way I have done, to feel trapped and isolated by mental health problems and to not be able to see a light at the end of the tunnel.

I would spend days on end in bed, unwilling, or even unable to move, for mental health can be so debilitating that it becomes physically disabling. I would hardly eat or drink, refuse to socialise, want to escape but not be able to as there was nowhere for me to go, knowing that I would always have to return to my room at the end of the day. It's a vicious cycle that, without help, is almost impossible to break.

The first big step for me was accepting, or as is often more difficult, realising that I was mentally unwell (after 2 very close suicide attempts). It took me a long time to do this. The days I spent lying in my bedroom, telling myself I was 'just bored', was me refusing to accept the reality that was my mental ill health.

I've seen a huge improvement in my mental health and I am a completely different person as a result. My mental health is still there, I think it always will be, but I can manage it to the extent that it doesn't affect my ability to function in day-to-day life. There are so many other people just like me who struggle with depression and that is why it is so important to raise awareness in order to prevent others from reaching the same horrible depths that I did.

I want to help create a world with good mental health for all and I hope my instagram has been helpful, or even inspiring this year.

Dave

Helmand Streets

Broken mind body and soul
Unforgiving Helmand heat
Beauty beyond these Sangin streets

Neville Johnson

Dave Radband

Afghanistan 2009, against a mud wall in Nadi Ali north, I was trying to control my emotions and get on with my mission. I had just shot another man dead outside a compound and I was juiced with a mix of adrenalin, relief and regret.

My family was worried that I wasn't going to come back the same. I remember saying, "I'll never tell them what things I did here. I'll never tell anybody." I'm not proud of some of the things I've seen or done, I'm just proud to be a Parachute Regiment soldier and be the best I can be.

My family was right. I didn't come back the same. I thought my war was over, but a few months later, back in the safety of my childhood

Dave

home surrounded by my adoring family, the dark secrets and all the demons emerged from my mind – like the Greeks from their hollow wooden horse, unrelenting in their destruction of ancient Troy.

The story of the Trojan horse, delivered as a gift but transporting lethal agents instead, has long served as an allegory for the destructive power of secrets – like the unaddressed guilt hidden in the minds of soldiers, repeated with every homecoming for thousands of years.

Wars' simple premise is like that Trojan horse, devastating those sent to do it and, ultimately, the society they return to when the war is done. The insidious damage is only made worse because wartime killing, a philosophically problematic act, has been left out of the global dialogue. After all, how can humanity's greatest civil crime, killing, become heroic in the context of war? There are practical considerations as well: will too much discussion of killing make soldiers hesitate or even rebel against protecting us from threats?

I, like many blokes, was able to contain my guilt while still on operations. But when I returned home, I brought the Trojan horse with me. It was there, in the calm of these 'safe' surroundings, that my guilt and shame overwhelmed me.

It was clear to my family that I was deeply troubled. I went to my GP, we tried everything, but nothing seemed to help, and I was unable to find any peace in civilian life.

I *HAD* to admit I needed help before I started to find peace with myself.

Sangin Valley's sunset peace
This foreign landscape a thing of beauty
A sunset I will remember
My thoughts my memories beyond those hills
Everything so insignificant
Feeling calm
Feeling content
This moment don't last
The sun burns out
The night regains its throne
Peace in the valley
If only for a while

Neville Johnson

Enplaning at Ft Bragg 1996, Bragg has an airbase
as part of the complex called Pope AFB. The
'FT' on the tail denotes it's from Pope/Bragg.

At the time this was the largest airborne drop since WW2, over 6,500 of us jumping over 6 hours, all at night. It's the only time I've been genuinely fearful for my life when jumping. The US T10 parachute wasn't great and the reserve was atrocious.

Author

Fort Bragg, North Carolina, 1996

Darren Roberts

Waiting

If there's one thing you do in the military, it's an enormous amount of hurrying up to wait. Of course for me I viewed this as an enormous waste of 'my' time, and took it all extremely personally. There were at least 6,000 better things I could've been doing - all of them nothing to do with where I was.

Looking back now of course, what I could've done instead of being all pissed off at what seemed like a lot of hurrying up and wait - was understand that was part of the job. Any movement of large amounts of troops takes time, a lot of time.

Not only that but I could rehearse what I needed to do in my head, check my kit again - and again. But I was too busy being impatient and frustrated at what I viewed as a creaking top heavy autocracy (which of course the military is) instead of trying to seek opportunity in any situation I was in - to be better.

The saying goes that youth is wasted on the young, and at the time I certainly had all the answers and very few questions. Of course the truth was very far from that, I knew nothing - was my time wasted doing some of the things? Yes totally. Did we do some utterly pointless things? Absolutely yes, it's the green military - that's like complaining about sand at the beach. If I didn't like it I should have done selection to do cool shit, had a beard and a plethora of non issue kit.

Patience and humility was something I was sorely lacking, and it's only now I can look back and understand that. Patience and humility can lead you on a much more fulfilling path, one that has empathy with the capacity to build new lasting friendships. Yep, there was a fuck tonne of 'hurry up and wait' - but is that such a bad thing if it gave us time?

Because in the end,

it's the one thing we all run out of.

Rob

Rob Creighton

The Stag

Chaos found in Stillness and anguish found in peace,

Three soulless shells causing grief that'll never cease,

The summer heat hastens stench and the living pour with sweat,

Who can imagine what the poor bride felt over the groom she never met.

Josh

We are different in all the same ways

Accept that people are different, maintain an even state of mind, and abandon your prejudices.

Judging people that are dissimilar to you is narrow minded, and in its rawest form it will get you killed. If you ever find yourself injured in hospital, on the battlefield, or need someone to pull you out of the hole when it hits the fan, will you refuse that help based on your own prejudice? If you truly would, you need to take a long hard look at yourself and get that fixed!

We don't care if you're male, female, gay, straight, of colour, an immigrant, or whatever else you can think of!

If you're shooting in the same direction as we are,

you're family until proven otherwise.

Darren Roberts
Attention to detail

For me, how someone does the little things tells me all I need to know about how they do the big things. The little things could be the elastic bands on your container before jumping, batteries charged with spares for equipment - it can also be understanding the nuances of the emotions and feelings of a loved one.

Failing to notice what is right in front of us emotionally, whether in ourselves or others is possibly the most important detail of all. Taking that 5 secs to stop what I'm doing to actually listen to what my daughter has to say, look her in the eye and being engaged in her moment. You can't get that back once you've missed it.

Being able to triage what's actually important in life is a total minefield - there are moments, times and events with my wife and daughter I will never get back. Through selfishness, ignorance, anxiety, depression and fundamentally failing to apply the very principals I would tell others about. I could not see what was in front of me. The little things, the moment, eye contact, a touch on the hand or shoulder - acknowledge the 'now' to notice others and yourself.

There is nothing bigger than the little things,

Don't let them slip by.

Abseiling out of a
Seaking somewhere in
Bosnia. Not to be
confused with 'fast
roping' which we did
out of Chinooks and
Pumas with a 20-30ft
thick rope you simply
held on to.

Author

Abseiling meant you can deploy from much higher in
the hover, and you would have your bergen slung
beneath you. The more horizontal you are the
faster you go, idea being to brake at the last
minute before you hit the deck.

Darren Roberts

Watching predator was
a seminal experience for me.

The jungle is, as everyone knows, a complete bag of fuck where anything and everything is designed to kill you or implant flesh eating beasties into you that eat their way out of you weeks later. All in what feels like a sauna. The one thing that wasn't life threatening - the ability to quote on demand in any situation something from Predator.

If our patrols met up in the jungle for whatever reason, whilst we went firm - you'd quote something to them. *"If it bleeds, we can kill it"* in faux Arnie voice, and as the other patrol moved off someone would whisper "stick around" as we stayed firm.

Cooking some dehydrated rat pack vomit, of course someone would say, *"This stuff will make you a god damned sexual Tyrannosaurus, just like me."* When waiting for some poor fucker trying to get the HF to work, *"call in position and situation. Get Con Op on the hook"*. Quoting these deadpan to each other, effortlessly, and at the most bizarre times is the sort or irreverent morale booster that keeps us going.

Humour and humility in the most extreme and dire places keeps you sane, things hurt a little less. When the helicopter came, it was the money shot,

"Get To Da Choppa"

Belize, Central America, 1995, author

Josh

Ace Of Iron Apparel

"Between stimulus and response, there is a space.
In that space is the power to choose our response"
– Viktor Frankl.

Gallows Humour

A common question people ask not only of veterans and people who serve in the military, but those in the emergency services too. Is why is your sensor of humour so messed up? To understand the phenomenon of dark humour you must dig into the psyche of it.

For people like us who see death on a regular basis, who have been over exposed to traumatic situations so unique they're difficult to explain, humour often becomes the only sane way to make sense of it all. It is statistically proven that the best human response to trauma is humour. We become so used to talking about death and messed up situations that we become desensitised to the meaning, and that's where dark humour originates.

Dark humour should not be labelled 'offensive' and you should not feel awkward or fearful about sharing that humour regardless of the subject. Because if it's funny, it's funny. People are so inverted into the importance of their own feelings in today's society that they shield themselves from everything even remotely offensive. As a consequence, their reactions to these statements are often as extreme as the first time they ever heard it. Ignore these people, for they are not worth your time, although do not respond aggressively.

It is not their fault for not choosing that
line of work.

Instead,
do what you do best and laugh.

Unknown location, sometime in the mid 90's, dug
in somewhere in shite weather!

Author

My Ink

Engraved in my skin
Imprinted in my mind
Burned into my soul
Forgotten for a while
Until now

Neville Johnson

Change

I'm not him no more
That version ceased to exit
The loved one you once knew
Departed into the Sangin night
Consumed by the Helmand Valley
Evolved into something new
Changed into something more
A change of choice
Change essential to life

Neville Johnson

Gut wrenching upturning feeling
Breathing deep to release it
Trying to focus on each breath
Attempting to focus on something else
Anything but this will do
This feeling I hate the most
Trying to keep my mind busy
Maybe if I'm distracted it will fade away
Refuse to look it in the eye
Aggression's dark desire to take control
Anger bleeding into my veins
Internal struggle in my mind

Struggle to control my breathing
Anxiety boiling filling my gut
Slowly taking over taking control
Clenching my fists I stand up
Resisting fighting not giving up
Out of the shadow she appears
Placing her hands on my shoulder
Her soft voice killing the white noise
Seeing the hope in her eyes
You can fight this
We can stop this
Her voice of hope for my soul
Anxiety slowly dying away
My angel my saviour
Not leaving my side

Neville Johnson

PX4 jump, 1990's, could be Hankley Common DZ.

Author

The Journey Is Long

In all honesty this section is one in which means the most to me. Every other section is a core part of who we are, and who we aspire to be, but for some reason this one strikes the most emotion in my soul. The very thought of this notion stabs deep within me, and is essentially the core driver for us progressing with DEVSOC. We use this phrase throughout our community and we have never really put pen to paper. The words exist on paper for everyone to see, but the emotion that this phrase references already exists within each and every DEVSOC Member, and that's why I believe it's so important.

The journey is long, longer than we'll ever know. For us, and for all, the "journey" can be anything. It's a highly subjective term for whatever path of life you are on. Wether it's a difficult course at work, a complete change in life direction, or an issue that you think may seem trivial to others, but you are finding hard to deal with. These are all *the* journey. They are all as equally as important as the other. For one person, their current struggles may come in the form of not being awarded their 100th gold medal. For another, it may be the act of leaving the house and tidying up. Both are equally important, subjectively. It doesn't matter where you are on your current journey, I say current as there will be many journeys that we travel upon in our times, it matters that you realise you are not alone.

We are all in this together, at least at DEVSOC. We are here for you, it doesn't matter if you're climbing Everest, or going to the shop for some milk. We're here to support you on whatever it is you're struggling with. We aren't superhuman conquerors who have done the unthinkable, we're just dudes who want to be there for others, and who will be there when you need us. There is absolutely nothing that will stop us from being there for you. We will shut our operations side down for the weekend if we find out someone is truly in need. If you need a chat, we are here. If you need a place to stay, we will do our utmost to figure something out. And that's why I believe in DEVSOC so much. We aren't a clothing company, we aren't an online retailer, we're a community of like minded souls who want to support others when the going gets tough, we want to be the voice in your head that says "keep going", we want to be the people who inspire the best in others. That's why we do this, and that's why we won't stop.

Perspective is a wild thing. For one person this might seem like an over the top expression, but for another who is in the midst of a crisis, it could be the thing that saves them, and that's who we're talking to. If you're in a good place today, great. Be grateful, and share the love. If you're in a bad place today, reread this and realise that there are many people like who you are in the same position, you just don't know it. Reach out to someone, give a loved one a call, if that's too much and you truly want an ear to listen, send our Instagram a DM. We don't judge, we don't berate, we don't preach advice. We'll listen. Listen to what is wrong, what is going on, and what you think you can do to fix it.

We're big believers that we can all help ourselves in numerous ways, sometimes that works, sometimes it doesn't. If you have to reach out for help, it's ok. There's nothing wrong with that. Most likely, the person you're talking to has experienced the same thing that you're dealing with. Swallow pride, get help. That's the most impressive thing a human can do - admit they need help and seek it. Trust us, we've been there.

Although a lonely path, it's one that you can take others on if you wish. And that's what we're building at DEVSOC. A group of people who'll congratulate you when you do well, who'll help you get better when you don't do well, and who wants to do this, not those who are forced to. There is no "You & Us", there is only "Us". A long road that can be not only endured, but enjoyed. We're all learning along it, it never ends, and we should be grateful for that. When we truly start to learn how long it is, it can be scary. But it's cool, we're all in this together.

The journey is long isn't just words on a screen, it's a philosophy for us. No marketing tripe, no hard-selling, no subscribe to X for more info. If you are in need and don't know where to turn, get in touch and we will help.

The journey is long, let's ride it together.

DevSoc

THE
DEVELOPMENT
SOCIETY

Lee Davies

From dust

Something great happened to me yesterday.

At about 3PM, I got fired from my job that had, until very recently, been hinting at equity in the company; a high five-figure income earned largely from home suddenly scratched down to zero. A few hours later, my roommate told me he was moving out. Thirty days from today, my reliable source of income and the routine I'd fallen into with my housemate will be no more. Someone else will be sharing my space, and I'll have to figure out where the next check is coming from or it won't come at all.

My first reaction, understandably, was the usual amalgam of shock, fear, and anger that accompanies this sort of out-of-left-field, routine-shattering, destabilising news. I'd helped this company post record profits the last quarter, and there was no actual reason for the firing other than the CEO bristling at the fact she'd hired somebody more talented than her. So the firing didn't just make zero sense; it was downright against the best interests of the business. And just the day before, my roommate had been talking about buying new patio furniture for the deck. So his announcement that he was taking over a friend's lease in a different part of town struck me as damn near a betrayal. Nonetheless, over the course of the next couple hours, that fear and resentment turned into excitement.

But what's so great – or even *good* – about being sent packing by your employer and forced to find a new lodger?

Let's back up a sec.

For the past few months, I'm embarrassed to say, I've been in a rut. The chief representative of the DevSoc California branch has, for several weeks now, been stuck in a morass of self-doubt and unfulfilling work; of missed PT sessions and too much booze; of chasing girls instead of goals. To my eternal shame and regret, I contributed approximately 25 minutes of meditation to our January goals and roughly the same number of calories burned. My creative output has been next to nil, my energies, instead, going to my relatively lucrative, but utterly unfulfilling day job and dating apps. At the risk of losing any remaining sympathy my esteemed reader might have for me or my situation, I've largely been prone to carrying a lot of lean muscle and very little fat no matter what I eat, and have tended, rather luckily, towards falling upwards career-wise, or at the very least landing on my feet when it comes to making money. So I've never had to bust my ass at the gym to look appealing to the opposite sex, nor had to truly commit myself professionally to make ends meet.

But I have never been happy.

Sure, there have been fleeting moments of triumph or, more ubiquitously, of carnal satisfaction; the dopamine hit of a little self-gift-giving with a nice watch or a terrific pair of leather shoes or a new pistol. There've been nights out with friends, and European vacations; desert trips in 4x4 vehicles and lucky nights out at bars. But what has eluded me for most of my life is that enduring, fortifying happiness that comes from chasing one's destiny; of knowing that you're where you're meant to be; that your cause is noble and you're pursuing it doggedly.

To put it harshly but fairly, I've led something of a low-effort life. So despite making more money than I have in a long time (from home, no less!), living in a sunny, desirable neighbourhood in Los Angeles, and being at least hip-deep in female affection at a given moment, I had been dying inside for a long time.

"Hardships often prepare ordinary people for an extraordinary destiny."

C.S. Lewis

My upbringing was, *ahem*, tumultuous, to say the least. A child of bitter divorce, changing cities and countries the way other families changed hairstyles. Seven different schools by the time I was seventeen and the accompanying social reboot, sometimes in languages I didn't yet speak. Savage parental abuse on one side; complete abandonment on the other. Drug and alcohol abuse pervaded as well; nervous breakdowns were commonplace. Perhaps most insidiously, my father's own bitterness at the trajectory of his career robbed me of a young man's optimism; of his willingness to charge a hill in spite of the looming threat of a Hun machine gun nest.

Something was always in the way; something was always happening *to* me. Moving countries; military enlistments; overdoses; the birth of a child; somebody's mental breakdown. Being thrown in jail at my Dad's behest; being excommunicated from my city; my friends; my family. Letting them back into my life, despite my better judgment, only to be subjected again to the same dysfunction that had characterised and reigned over their existences.

The end result was never feeling rested; never feeling ready to take on the world. **I had been putting out fires for so long, I had missed the years where I was supposed to be feeding mine.**

After responding to not one but *three* separate heroin overdoses in my family, I had had enough.

I cut ties and vowed to rebuild my life; rebuild *myself*. But that's easier said than done when you've been raised by wolves.

I had been walking around with deep, raw streaks of unbridled jealousy and rage coursing beneath the surface; unwittingly informing my reactions to the successes of friends and undermining my romantic relationships. The psychotic, merry-go-round vacillations of ebullient parental praise and devastating abuse lead me to constant comparisons of myself to people who'd achieved more in their lives than me, at times ravaging what remained of my self-esteem. And until recently, I was possessed of a singular and insidious belief that surely some cosmic relief was on its way. Surely I was owed *something*; some reprieve from the constant gut checks and dick kicks and continuous geographic upheaval and familial psychodrama. I was owed at least that, right? Wrong.

I am thirty two years old, and nobody is coming to help me. And that's a damned freeing realisation.

Since my personal epiphany a few years back, I've been largely coasting, removing bad habits and scrubbing out the dead tissue of infectious emotional trauma where I could, but failing to realise that I needed to be *building* something in its stead, or the same psychospiritual pathogens would simply fill the void and wreak havoc again.

I took jobs that didn't mean anything to pay the rent on a place that isn't the home I'll raise my family in; spent emotional capital on things that wouldn't sustain me for the journey of life ahead. I let my choices be informed by fears – not making rent; being alone; feeling too much – rather than my dreams – a career in the arts; the loving company of a good woman; a well-developed soul with which to weather life's storms.

My goals – professional screenwriting, acting on stage and in film – have a fairly murkily-defined career trajectory, but it damn sure doesn't involve 60+ hour workweeks in a not-even-tangentially related industry. So the "loss" of this job isn't a loss at all. It's an unshackling; a license to forego the golden handcuffs of relative comfort, and a grim, liberating reminder of one simple truth: only the mission matters. Everything else is a distraction that will cost you your life. For me, that mission is finding success in film and television. For you, that might mean buying a house, or bringing a company to an IPO, or finishing grad school. But no matter what it is, you will not get the time back that you spend on anything else. So strip away everything else. Don't be afraid of starting from nothing. *All come from dust, and to dust we return.*

Beneath the ashes of volcanic eruption are singularly fertile soil. Similarly, in the vacuum left by the explosion of some of my life's erstwhile constants, I am free to plant whatever I wish. New habits and alliances can be formed; new goals decided on and new courses plotted for them. Where I was waking up and tucking into half a million Slack DM's from my jittery CEO, I will have peace and clarity. Where my words would be wasted on sales copy and pithy tweets on behalf of a company in whose success I didn't share, they will once again serve me. Where my health and energy were spent ensuring that the company was ending the day in the best place it could, I will instead spend that energy on my own mental and physical solidity. I will be beholden only to myself, with only myself to rely on. It will be as it should be.

If you're very lucky, there might be some people you can depend on if everything goes tits up; a kindly grandmother who'll mail you the rent if you're in a jam or a wife that will support you. But for many of us, the only tools we have are our own cracked hands and the friendships we've forged through our better actions.

More importantly, on the journey of a life meaningfully lived, the only respite we can ever truly rely on is our faith in the nobility of our cause. The canteen may run dry; the fire may grow cold. The sun may set; the heavens might open up. But if your cause matters, you'll take another step. It doesn't even have to matter anywhere beyond the space between your ears. As long as it matters to *you*, you'll find a few more wisps of gas in the tank; find the strength to go a few more miles. Most importantly, you'll avoid the toxic curse that is regret.

It's fair to say that I may well be the most dysfunctional of the DevSoc cadre. So I feel best poised to tell you, dear reader, that no matter how desperate the circumstances, no matter how rife with existential dread the hole you find yourself in may be, there's a way out if you keep digging. I'll be damned if I know where the tunnel leads, but I do know it doesn't lead to regret.

I wish I could be writing this from the mountaintop. I wish, truly, that I could tell you that this is the course of action that had already worked for me; that the glory and the goods are sitting right next to me on this sunny peak if only you follow my simple steps.

But I can't. I'm on the same fucking road as you, buddy. My pack is just as heavy. My boots are as muddy; my bones as tired.

But we're on our way.

DevSoc

Lee Davies

Build your mind,
like you build your body.

I recently purchased a copy of Letters From A Stoic by Seneca. Amazed that I haven't read it before now, I dove straight in. It's simply amazing that these words were written over 2000 years ago, the insights, the prose, the way Man's trials and tribulations don't seem to change, no matter how much the world around Him changes, blows my mind.

As always, all that I read is taken with a pinch of salt. It must be. There's no way you can take all that is read as gospel, for doing so creates an air of giddy excitement that belongs to a novice. This is not saying that it is wrong to be excited by words written on paper, for I am truly excited by the words I have read. I try to apply the guiding philosophy of "trust but verify" - read other sources of contradicting views of the author, ask questions like - who really was Seneca? It's all very easy to immediately fall into the words head-over-heels, but a certain amount of restraint is called for in verifying these written letters. Thankfully this translation of Seneca's Letters includes a prologue by Robin Campbell, which builds out this point exactly. It allows you to arm yourself with the knowledge that is most often overlooked by readers of classical texts, who the Hell was the author? Well, I'll leave that for you to decide. For it is entirely a subjective view, and projecting my view onto you would not be effective, or at all needed. We all have our own Directing mind, let's use it.

I've read many of the Letters, but there is one I cannot seem to shake from my thoughts. In my eyes, there is nothing that rings truer, especially in today's modern society of travelling, entertainment, and a distinct lack of investing in one's mind. The premise of the point is simple - "Where you arrive does not matter so much as to what sort of person you are when you arrive there".

How many times have you heard a person state "I cannot WAIT for my holiday", the underlying truth to their statement being that it will somehow "fix" them, or make their world okay again. But it won't, and it doesn't. The same person will return from a brief respite of their core being to the same feelings of overwhelming anxiety, 'directionless-ness' and everything else that they were trying to escape. A change in our physical surrounding can do nothing for these thoughts, we can think that they will, but it's simply not possible.

Whatever your destination you will be followed by your failings. Here is what Socrates said to someone who was making the same complaint:

'How can you wonder your travels do you no good, when you carry yourself around with you? You are saddled with the very thing that drove you away'

If you have self-deprecating thoughts, negative mindsets, corrosive mannerisms and behaviours, a "spiritual" trip to Bali will not solve them. In order to put these right, you must first acknowledge them. No one is immune from this, we all have negative behaviours, whether they're surface level in our being or buried in the depths of it. It's our job as people who want to be better, not only for ourselves but for the people around us. For what are we truly? Are we selfish beings who only exist to appease our own lives? I don't think so. We're all here together, and as I've stated before "The journey is long", let's ride it together. Let's put ourselves second, or even third. There is time for us to build ourselves, when we are alone in the morning and evening, but who will help others when they are in need of it? Do not wait for others to show kindness, or whatever you wish them to display, offer it first. Be the first to make that step towards a better world, even if your world is the block where you live or a family home. Only then can others lead in your footsteps and take the same stance. Quiet confidence is what is needed.

Cities, woodland, a foreign country, an all-inclusive hotel - these things do nothing for our mind. They can soothe it for a short while, but it does nothing for our lives. It is like applying a plaster when a tourniquet is needed. This can seem like a juxtapositional argument, I am not saying that being outdoors in the fresh air does no good - it does a world of good and we should all aim to get outside more. But being outside by itself does not address whatever problems we all face. It's what you do whilst outside that matters, staring at your phone in the woods scrolling endlessly through social media will not help. But sitting, thinking, meditating, breathing, working your mind, might.

Think of the amount of time we, as a general population in 2019, spend on building and fortifying our minds. It is minuscule. For the mind is what I believe, is the single most important thing we possess, we spend a staggeringly small amount of time working on it. Imagine if you were to not spend any time building your body, it withers, grows (in an unhealthy manner), and becomes fraught with illness and injury. But we don't allow this to happen, generally, as it is on show - for the whole world to see. I agree building the body is of the utmost importance, but let us put the same focus and energies on building the mind as we do the body. I guarantee our lives will be richer for it.

I do not pass these words as gospel, nor do I pass them on from above a high perch. These are merely the thoughts I have whilst driving, drinking coffee, and thinking with my brain. Writing them down is one of the sanest things a person can do. I urge you all to think thoughts of your own, have arguments, form ideas, build a world for your mind where it is worked. Use your mind for what it is intended, not just to be sold things to by conglomerates.

DevSoc

Rob Creighton

H e a r t &

S o u l

With the kindest of souls and a sparkle in her heart that even the
stars envy.

For Emily

Lee Davies

Lee Davies

Let it rain

The "ebbs & flows", we talk about them a lot. But what does it really mean?

It's the Yin & Yang, the ups & downs, the to & fro of life. It's also more than that, it's about understanding when they hit, that they are supposed to happen that way, for it cannot happen any other.

In the simplest of terms: there are no ups without downs. It's a simple sentence, yet one which holds much more than six words and twenty-five characters. It's a modus operandi, an operating system of life.

When things are going your way, great. When they are going against you, great. It is meant to be like this: to seek constant happiness or "ups" is insanity. It does not exist. If you master the true essence of this conscious thought, you'll learn to appreciate life in a much clearer distillation. You can take a step back, take time to understand that the world moves in a wave-like motion, it isn't linear.

Without the sadness in our lives, there is no happiness. And without happiness, there is no sadness. They come as a pair. Not just "sadness" & "happiness" either; every single aspect of our life is entwined in this everlasting, constant, cyclical motion of ebbs & flows. We can't learn to control it, but we can learn to "let it go".

The harder you grasp onto the waves, the harder they are to keep in your hands. Learn to take a deep breath, open your mind, and let it go. Don't hold on. The more you hold, the further it moves away.

It is easy to write about, but it is difficult to put into practice. It could take 5 minutes, or it could take 50 years. There is no "right" time to start, so start today. There is no "right" amount of time to take, there is only the time that it will take you: your journey.

A real-life example of this can be applied to your working life. Assuming your working life consists of, at least, a small amount of thinking. If you sit down to write the answer to the problem you are solving, it will very likely escape you. The answer that you seek will not necessarily be available in your head, it may occur to you and then disappear. The answer is in your mind, you just need to find it. Stop. Do something that relaxes your mind, go on a walk, watch a film, and try to use the "back" of your brain to do the thinking. Your mind overcomes problems, jumps hurdles, and navigates treacherous courses when it is allowed to be free and move as it wishes. Don't hold it tight to your chest and be frustrated by a lack of answers on the paper. The answer is in your mind, it just has to rise to the surface and take form. Psychologically, you have 'access to all the resources that you need' and you just need to access them. Free your mind, create the space to access your inner resources.

I wrote this post in two halves, before this line, and after. In between, I had to take a short drive into town. As I left, as typical with the North East weather, it was a torrential storm. I took this time as a chance to reflect on what I'd just written. It turned out the same could be said for the weather eco-system we all abide by. The whole system is the sum of many parts: sun, rain, snow, sleet, hail, wind, and everything in between. If we only have one of these parts, it usually distills into an inhospitable landscape. Only sun and there is a desert. Only rain and there are monsoons. Only snow and, well technically another desert. To be in a "truly habitable" or "happy" landscape, we must endure all of these parts as they arrive. As the rain hammered against my 98 plate £200 Volvo, I considered this: "It rains because it must".

I challenge you today, for whatever is thrown your way: do your best to understand that it rains because it must. I shall do the same.

Trust your brain, trust your mind. Let it go, and it will all come back.

DevSoc

Lee Davies

Lee Davies

The diseconomy of scale

Throughout the course of our lives, we adjust perpetually to our circumstances – those of us faced with adversity grow accustomed to it; those of us blessed with good fortune in turn come to expect the frictionless existences which we lead. Neural pathways are flexed and forged and, to our eternal peril, obstacles scale accordingly. As such, things that might seem a trifle to us can send those inculcated to comfort into a tailspin.

And, dangerously, vice-versa.

It's fair to say that if you're reading this, you're likely somewhere in the middle, having the immense good fortune to be an English-speaker, in the West, able to afford a computer or cell phone. Congratulations, you're extraordinarily lucky, as am I. But it doesn't always feel that way. Without vigilance and gratitude, our relatively lightweight problems will fill to the space you allow them, and before you know it, molehills become unfathomable mountains. Leaving you, when the time comes that you're faced with some real shit, hopelessly underprepared.

Unlike my DevSoc comrade who recently wrote of sipping an Espresso in a cheery London cafe, I'm writing this in a Coffee Bean (an American chain) somewhere in mid-city Los Angeles, whiling away the time it takes for my vehicle's alignment to get done. As auto shops don't typically occupy LA's most desirable zip codes, suffice it to say the crowd here is a bit more varied than my esteemed colleague's London bistro. To my left, there's a maybe-homeless, 60-something African American woman in a blue wig who orders, simply, hot water. To her left is a mentally-disabled woman of about 35, compulsively eating chewing gum. I feel saddened, but not existentially moved. I do what any of us does –

avert my gaze, tuck into my laptop, and try to ignore the smells of unwashed bodies.

It's only after another, more affluent woman comes in, exits, and returns that I'm reminded of something seismic, something I'd paved over with years of banal existential ease. She approaches the counter, her frappa-whatever in an outstretched hand, as though carrying a full diaper. "Did you guys put the vanilla powder in this?" she inquires, with the same suspicion and disgust as someone asking if they'd swapped the whipped cream with horse jizz. "Um, no, we just use the regular mix," comes the obvious answer. "Well it doesn't taste like it. You guys clearly have no idea what you're doing," she spits, before letting out a disgusted Ugh, leaving the drink on the counter, and storming out, her day clearly rattled by something as preposterously insignificant as a $5 coffee milkshake being too sweet.

OK, now I get it. The pungent aroma of the homeless lady near me becomes all the more acrid in the void the affluent young woman has left. The absurdity of comparative misfortune crystallizes, and I realize, this lady's whole fucking day has changed because of a coffee. She didn't even ask politely if they could re-make it. She just stormed out, quivering with righteous indignation. Clearly absurd, right?

But then I realize, holy shit – what similarly indefensible transgressions have I made in the course of the last week? How comfortable have I gotten, and how disproportionately have my problems scaled? What minutia have I gotten far too upset about? The service was too slow at the restaurant? Traffic sucked a little more than usual? I missed happy hour? I was suddenly horrified.

Then I flashed back to my life 5 years ago, when my problems carried the weight of life and death, and I was awash with a beautiful clarity. I used to have a fairly high-stakes occupation, the nature of which I can't disclose on an open forum, but whose day-to-day operations carried a near-perpetual threat of physical violence and robbery. As such, smaller problems became just that – small. Wondrously, magnificently, insignificantly small. When I went back to the world of normies, I was perpetually puzzled by the shit people got upset about. And yet, years later, the siren song of bitching about trivia calls as sweetly as ever.

As many veterans of combat arms can attest, when you're dealing in extremes, when you're gambling with your life and the lives of others, when the consequences are about as high stakes as they can get, the little shit doesn't matter. You think that homeless lady with the blue wig gives a fuck if her frapp arrives a little too sweet? You think a dude who's spent ten hours in a dick-dragger of a gunfight, trying to guide close air support while 7.62 rounds pepper the walls around him gives a rat's ass if the beer isn't cold when he gets back?

The answer is, almost without exception, "Fuck No."

It's only when we become used to the soft, easy lives that we're so easily seduced by that these trifles become grave. And God help you when some real shit goes down. If that lady was at an 8 out of 10 because of a coffee, imagine what she'd be at if she got mugged, or had a family member get sick, or got fired, or if any one of a litany of real problems came her way.
Imagine what number you'd be at. Hopefully not as high as Ms. Frappuccino, but would you stay as wavy as Mrs. Blue Hair or Johnny JTAC? Probably not.

So what can we learn? What action can we take to inoculate ourselves from the disease that is the overabundance comfort? Gratitude and hardship. One of the core tenets of DEVSOC is, "Get Humbled." Do some shit that makes you feel small. Lift weights 'til you throw up. Feed the homeless. Climb a mountain. Test your mettle against something you're genuinely unsure about your ability to navigate and prevail.

The other component, I'd humbly submit, is an expression of gratitude. Whether it's mentally, to a journal, as part of a meditation, take time to reflect on the blessings in your life, no matter how fundamental or basic they seem. You're not in the street. You're not taking IDF (at least, not right now, if you're reading this). You're alive, and you're here. Whatever struggles you've got pale in comparison to those of the   blue-haired homeless lady, or a Yazidi being rounded up by ISIS, or a Kurd getting rat-fucked by our Cheeto-In-Chief, or any of the millions of people whose problems dwarf yours. Keep that shit in perspective. Weigh the obstacles against the globe's as a whole, and ask yourself – is this worth my energy to stress over? Your problems will seem far, far less daunting, and far more actionable. And the good shit will seem all the better by comparison. And if for whatever reason your circumstances aren't what you'd like them to be, remember, we humans are blessed with the infinite possibility for change.

So keep calm, give thanks, get humbled, and enjoy your fucking Frappuccino.

DevSoc

Early LLP jump, mid 90's. This was a brand new parachute at the time and I thought it was a massive step forward compared to the PX4.

Abseiling out of a Seaking somewhere in
Bosnia.

National Arboretum

Everything that is old, is new again....

You often hear that life goes in cycles and that history repeats itself. Staring down the barrel of 50 years old, this has been my experience my adult life.

As much as we need to progress and move forward, we also need to be students of history - and not the history written by the victors. We all like to think we are innovators, originators - however the truth is that someone somewhere has probably done it or said it before. If you go back far enough, you'll find truth, context and relevance from 50 years ago to 3,000 years ago.

My issue pocket knife is still going strong 30 years since it was issued to me. It's been looked after, and even sent back to Eggington's in Sheffield for an MoT. It still serves it's purpose and serves it well. Sometimes the old way, isn't a bad way to do something because they got it right the first time, simple works.

In a digital instantly consumable world,

it's nice to have something that's analogue,

real and is still like new 30 years later.

G.I.(S)L. 1989 ↑
7340−99−975−7402

OIL THE
JOINTS

Exercise somewhere
hot, you see it was
cool to fold cuffs
even in the mid
90's

Darren Roberts

Military Slang

Like any close knit tribe or community, the military has its own language. From personal experience, this allows you to immediately strike up a conversation with someone who you don't even know, might not be from the same service or the even the same country. In typical military style, this is all grounded in humour, irony and satire.

Whilst this possibly seems to be just about banter, it can also serve a much more serious utility - interoperability. The shortest route to someone is humour, so if you can connect with someone by speaking a similar language along with the humour - you can slot right in.

Whilst there are some idiosyncrasies between the services and even within the services themselves, front line units can and do share this common language.

Over the next few pages, the various terms and their meanings are explained - some obvious, others less so!

Stag (on)

Sentry or guard duty, either on an established military base or out in the field on operations. 'Stagging on' covers most situations where you are relatively stationary watching something or watching out for something.

"I'm having to stag on with the kids at a birthday party mate, I can't come out"

"Where is *insert name of oppo here*?"

"He's got to stag on at a family thing"

Chin strapped

Extremely tired, so tired that you are hanging off your helmet 'chin strap'.

"I'm absolutely chin strapped mate".

"Been dragged all around the shops, totally chin strapped"

Recce

To observe something discreetly beforehand, such as a military objective or a pub's suitability.

"I recce'd that pub last week, full of fit birds".

Marking Time

Relates to parade square drill move of marching on the spot, i.e going nowhere.

"We're just here marking time until we find out what's going on".

You spend a significant amount of the working week 'marking time' waiting to find something out.

Its significance usually inversely proportional to the amount of time you had to wait to get it.

Nosebag

Food

Walt

Someone who massively exaggerates and or tells lies

Blag

Convince someone that you need something or need to do something - which you 100% do not need or need to do legitimately.

"I've blagged the afternoon off work"

Chit

Refers to a piece of paper that affords the holder something,

"I've got a chit from the missus for a night out".

You do not want to head out on the piss with the blokes without securing one of these beforehand.

On The Biff

In the barracks with an injury or illness that may or may not be real. More likely not real. Definitely not real.

Babies Heads

Can refer to the old school 24 hour ration pack tin of steak & kidney pudding. More commonly refers to the thick tufts of gorse like

Author

Belize, mid 90's - looks like we've just finished a range live fire serial in the trees. We've got iron sights on instead of SUSAT's because 4x optics are useless in the jungle, as you can't see more the two foot in front of you.

grass on the Brecon Beacons which are made out of Adamntium steel and can snap an ankle instantly.

Benny Hat

A small woollen hat, very similar to one worn by 70's soap character called 'Benny' from Coronation Street.

Bull

Cleaning anything.

E&E

Escape & Evasion, often used in situations where you've failed to secure your chit for a night out.

Solider 1   "I thought you weren't coming out tonight?"

Soldier 2   "Yeah I know I fucking E&E'd it"

Can also refer to actually having to escape and evade an actual enemy in combat.

Pop Smoke

When it's time to leave a location quickly and unobserved through the cover of a smokescreen.

"I had to pop smoke in the pub as the missus walked in"

"I saw the RSM heading my way so I popped smoke"

Gobbling Rods

Knife, fork and spoon

Gimpy

7.62mm belt fed, fully automatic General Purpose Machine Gun. The mainstay of section level firepower for the last 1,500 years and still going strong. Weighs a fucking tonne, but will fuck shit up whether it's mounted on a vehicle, on a tripod in its sustained fire role or someone going full Rambo.

I went full Rambo once on exercise and got absolutely rinsed. Was worth it though.

Nails

Someone or something that is extremely 'hard'.

"That course was nails",

"The 5 miles of death is nails".

Gonk Bag

Military sleeping bag, or any sleeping bag anyone from the military ever encounters.

Bodge Tape

Thick black tape which fixes anything, anywhere, any time. 60% of all military equipment is held together by 32% bodge tape at any given time. From helmets to aircraft. Fact.

Belize, mid 90's - we've got the Gimpy set up in its Sustained Fire role for a live firing serial.

Author

Knock Off

Finish work for the day

Cabbage

Someone who absolutely loves soldiering, but too much. Like an airsofter who is an actual soldier, usually has a DPM duvet cover. Or MTP as it is now, or whatever it is. You're all crows. Fuck off.

Skivvies

Underwear

Minging

Not nice, something which is awful. Food, people, tours, countries - everything and anything can be minging.

Gopping

As above, but usually said by a Marine

Hanging

Something which is also awful

Threaders

Same as chin strapped, but likely to be said by a Marine - probably whilst naked in a bar, and having been kicked out of the bar is now struggling to secure transport home (due to being naked). "I'm threaders today as last night I had to yomp home naked"

Redders

Extremely hot.

"This Jungle is fucking redders"

Only said by marines, everyone else says, "yeah it's fucking hot"

Thin Out

To disperse, go away - again yet another marine only saying.

Zero Alpha

The Officer Commanding's call sign on the battle net, but mainly refers to wife or girlfriend.

Sunray

As above, but used by old sweats because I don't think it's supposed to be used anymore.

Essence

Extremely nice, fantastic and tends to be people or things - likely said by a Marine. This place is 'essence', she is total 'essence'.

Hoofing

Same as essence, but usually referring to a situation i.e that night out was hoofing! Usually said by a Marine, because it involved a naked bar.

Wet

What Marines call a cup of tea

Brew

What everyone else in the english speaking military world calls a cup of tea that isn't a Marine.

Scoff

Food

Scran

What marines call scoff

Doss Bag

As per gonk bag, it's a sleeping bag.

Slug

What marines call sleeping bags

Grot

What marines call personal space in barracks or on ships

Pad

A house where married people live

Tea Bomb

Large industrial size flask of tea which contains enough for everyone to have cup

Brass

Empty casing of live or blank rounds. "We need to pick all this brass up".

Rupert

Officer

Oggin

To put something in the sea, it's lost, got rid of - something a Marine would say and frankly fuck knows why.

Racing Snake

Someone who is very fit, and very fast.

"He smashed his BFT, he's a right racing snake',

"who was the racing snake at the front?'

No one likes a racing snakes. Probably training for selection.

Secret Squirrel

Special Forces, MI5, MI6, SRR

Rat Pack(s)

Issue 24 hour ration packs

Gucci

High end kit, usually privately purchased that is very good at what it does - but can also refer to a newly issued innovative piece of kit or more likely another countries kit (usually better).

"We got issued these gucci boots, mega bits of kit"

Baltic

Extremely cold

Otters Pocket

Extremely wet

Bug out

Leave an area extremely quickly with little or no time to pack equipment. Can be during an operation,

"we had to bug out of that position",

but can also be applied to any situation you have to leave immediately,

"Time to bug out of this pub"

Bumped

Similar to having to bug out, but due to enemy contact, "We were set up having some scoff and got bumped".

Egyptian PT

Sleeping

Author

Northern Ireland, mid 90's, chest rigs were the epitome of ally - before they became tacticool 20 years later

Beer Tokens

Money

Brecon Point

A way of pointing at things with the whole hand in a 'karate chop' style when giving orders or instructions, connected to the Infantry Battle School, Brecon Beacons.

Can be seen in use in the supermarket, giving directions to a lost civilian, children's parties when explaining what they should or shouldn't do, parent teacher evenings when explaining to the teacher why they're wrong about your kid.

Essentially any situation that requires instruction to be given and followed. It's a one way conversation.

Military Confetti

Shrapnel from explosive devices such as grenades.

Shrapnel

The coin change everyone keeps in their ashtray in their car or wherever on their person.

"Have you got any shrapnel for the car park?"

Not to be confused with actual 'shrapnel' from the explosive fragmentary metal from actual explosives. That would be stupid.

Flashed

Lost temper,

"Yeah he wound me up and I flashed".

Also 'getting someone to flash' through relentless banter is often the goal, it means you won. Which is the main thing.

Social Hand Grenade

Someone who is a nightmare on a night out having had 'a' drink, causes havoc and has to be constantly watched, usually gets everyone into a fight. All Marines are social hand grenades, whether drink is involved or not.

Wanking Chariot

Bed

Rag Order

Refers to someone and or their kit at the end of an op or exercise in a debilitated and/or untidy state.

"I was in absolute rag order after that".

Can also refer to someone or group of soldiers who do not present themselves or manage themselves well in the field. Usually hats (non airborne).

"Mate did you see the state of that lot? Absolute rag mate"

More often than no though, it's most commonly used when on a shopping expedition with a significant other,

"All afternoon in Ikea mate, I was in fucking rag'.

In Clip

Similar to 'Rag Order' but more to do with pain.

"I was in clip at the end of that 10 miler"

"We were all in clip on that patrol"

NoDuff

Not an exercise, this is real. i.e 'no duff' medical emergency whilst on exercise, as someone has actually hurt themselves.

Probably someone from the rear echelon who fell over their incorrectly fitted strap for their weapon, injuring themselves - and as their helmet was also likely undone have caused themselves or others further injury.

'66

Light Anti Tank Weapon 66mm

Sky Pilot

Military chaplain

Pants

Poor Admin No Tactics, someone or something that has no point and is not good. "This pub is pants".

Digging Tools

Knife, fork, spoon.

Cook House

The area where the food is served and eaten on a military base

Wagon

Can be any military vehicle from a 110 Landrover to an actual HGV 'Wagon' and even armoured vehicle.

"Right back to the wagons lads and we'll make a move"

Bomb Up

Load your magazines and yourself with a significant amount of ammunition.

De-Bomb

Having spent a large amount of time 'bombing-up' with a significant amount of ammunition, you then need to put it all back because it's not been used.

Some twat always looses a round.

Tab

Tactical Advance to Battle, moving across long distances at speed, carrying significant weight to close with the enemy.

Also refers to anything that involves moving any distance on foot

Ginkel Heath DZ, nr Arnhem September 2019

for any reason. "This taxi isn't coming lads, fuck it shall we tab to the next place?".

Yomp

What Marines called 'Tabbing' - again, fuck knows why

Hat

A craphat, someone who is not Airborne. Para Reg call anyone who isn't Para Reg 'hats' even if the have their wings. Can also refer to something that is a bit shite, "that's such a hat thing to do".

Badged troopers in the SAS from the Para Reg even call other badged troopers 'hats' if they're not from Para Reg, true story.

Blades

Badged troopers on a sabre squadron of the SAS

Shakeys

Badged troopers on a squadron of the SBS, which only used to exclusively recruit from the marines.

Lid

Beret

Ally

Something which all soldiers strive for at all times and in all situations military related. How 'ally' you look is directly proportional to your perceived soldiering ability.

Special forces tend to the masters of 'allyness' due to extremely relaxed regulations on clothing and equipment in the field.

Allyness also saves lives - a well known and demonstrably true military fact.

Ghat

Personal weapon system, most enlisted soldiers goal with a 'ghat' is hide one that is left unattended as it should be such a rare thing - especially if it's a rupert.

If you're around REMFs then there's ghats fucking everywhere along with all their kit, so it gets boring really quickly hiding their stuff as it's most of their stuff.

Giving It (Big) Licks

Putting a huge amount of effort in, whether that be during a Tab, a section attack, drinking, telling a story or all of those things combined.

"He was giving it big licks about how he was going to crush that course - but didn't"

"Alright mate calm down, no need to be giving it all the licks"

"I gave it big licks up that hill"

Bivvy

Taken from 'Bivouac', personal shelter in the field, usually made with a poncho and bungees. Guaranteed some crow will trip over it, causing it to collapse on you in the rain at 2am soaking you and your kit.

Bivvy area is the location the team, section or entire company set up in the field to operate from.

"Lets bivvy up here"

Also refers to any other scenario where you need to stay somewhere such as on the piss on a new location,

"Have we got anywhere to bivvy up tonight?"

"No mate we're drinking through"

Basha

What marines call a bivvy. Because Marines.

Monk On

In a bad mood, referring to how a monk with the hood up and arms crossed looks. Not happy.

"He's got a right monk on because he's been dicked with gate guard at the weekend".

Doom On

Similar to monk on and used in same situations.

Buckshee

Free

Diffy

Missing, can be a thing or person.

"He went diffy after the last pint".

"Fuck I'm diffy some gloves, I'll get billed for them fuck sake".

REMFs

Rear Echelon Mother Fuckers, people that do not go out into the field or on patrol. Usually support staff, logistics, basically anyone who doesn't need to fire a weapon effectively.

Can be a complete liability in the field, the telly tubbies have better weapon handling skills, more tactical and situational awareness than a REMF. If they find themselves in the field with you, it's can be a disaster. If it can be lost, they will loose it (including themselves, vehicles).

"Has anyone seen the REMF?! Where the fuck is he!? We've only gone 50m how have we lost him already?!"

If it can be forgotten, they will forget it.

"I forgot the magazines for my gun"- what's more heinious in this situation, isn't that they have no way of using their weapon system, as they'd likely shoot you by accident, but they call it a 'gun'.

All of this though can be forgiven if they are a fucking ninja at what their actual job is. If the MT guy is some sort of savant when it comes to fixing wagons in the middle of nowhere with no kit or resources other than their own wizardry, he is nurtured and looked after by everyone like a delicate flower.

If they are shit at their actual job though....

Labrador, Newfoundland,
1994 or 1995, author

Humour and Humility

Words we often see and may even be part of your ethos. However they're just words, unless you actually live by them.

I know I don't know what the fuck I'm doing, at all. I have nothing sorted, rarely am I in control of what's happening. If anything I do actually seems to work, it's only born out of a catastrophic mistake, not some prescient yoda like quality of having my shit dialled.

Surely then, this is where humour & humility can help me out. That dark sense of humour squaddies are known for, finding humour to bring levity to even the most dire of situations. Why? Because the shortest distance between two people is humour.

So before I loose myself in a self absorbed epic stoic picture (monochrome of course) doing a blue steel that Seneca, Epictetus and Marcus Aurelius would have adopted me on the spot for - where's my humility? Telling you what to do isn't humble, however sharing my experiences (rightly and wrongly) may help show someone that they're not alone.

It's no fun being 150 miles from the nearest thing except bears in sub arctic Canada, wearing DPM in a snow covered tundra, having being told to be that most heinous of things - 'Semi Tac'.

So get the stupid goggles out.

Josh

On Humility

Humility can be defined as having a moderate or low view of ones self. Which in society's never-ending struggle to achieve 'perfect', is often mis-interpreted by those who 'appear' to be successful as counter productive. These people will always tell you that having a low view of yourself is never a good thing.

However, there is a reason why those who think that way do not operate at the higher tiers of this existence. Humility is an asset for self improvement that allows you to remain humble, and to not develop anger or frustration at life's losses. For that clouds you're judgment. Humility allows you to become a better human being... not perfect, just better, because 'perfect' is an impossible task.

Rest assured, if you do not remain humble,

life will quickly rectify that issue.

Lee Davies

Rob Creighton

Discipline

Discipline is not a random fleeting moment or drippy emotion, nor is it a thing you can simply pick up where ever you abandoned it. You can't use it like a crutch whenever you feel the urge to do things you have not readied for.

Discipline is not a materialistic accessory to adorn yourself in because it sounds good, looks good or ticks a box. It cannot be faked, falsified or feigned. Never pretend to be disciplined, you will be found out almost immediately.

Discipline is not free or simple; it is not easy and it is not for the feint hearted. Those who are meagre in their application and sloppy in their execution cannot tame it. It takes time, repetition and habit. But it can harnessed.

Discipline needs to be built; it needs to be built brick by brick, course by course until it's a big fucking impenetrable fortress. Your fortress.

Now, Don't be scared by discipline; Take hold of it and place it beside you. Arm yourself to the back teeth with it and move courageously forward with it.

Never stop moving forward with it.

Discipline will change you.

Lee Davies

C o u r a g e

It's often said that, "courage is not in the absence of fear but in spite of it", or for courage to come into action there must be the overwhelming presence of fear.

Courage is action & decision placed boldly in the face of pain, danger, uncertainty or intimidation. Courage is a positive reaction against a negative force. Simply put; it is Good versus Evil.

Often courage isn't like it is portrayed in literature or film. Real courage can be applied under hesitation and trembling limbs. The heart is strong, the head is willing but the physical 'doing' does not come naturally to the individual, who's shoulders on which the responsibility of action is bestowed.

If courage is ever required of you: God Speed.

Author

Darren Roberts

Forward, in all directions

What are my expectations, hopes or even goals with this book? Having been on my own mental health journey for many years, and now being in a position where I feel I am on the other side of that journey - I simply wanted to try and give something back. There are some fantastic people doing amazing things, social media can be a force for good - the amount of accounts out there with solid actionable advice is brilliant. That's why I've collated what I can in this book, so it doesn't get lost in the content graveyards of social media. Help is out there, it's all around and within reach, it won't be the MoD knocking on the door to help you - but we can sure as shit help each other.

Mental health, or more accurately a lack of mental health, is absolutely endemic in society. The fact that suicide kills more men under 50 in the UK than anything else is fucking ridiculous. Not cancer, heart disease, alcohol or a hundred other causes - suicide is the biggest killer of men under 50, and has been for a number of years. What does that say about us as a society?

This isn't a veteran issue, it's an issue for society as a whole - and help is not coming. Mental health services have been stripped to the bone by successive governments for as long as I can remember, and whilst correlation doesn't mean causation - it's very hard to ignore the lack of mental health resources with the poor state of mental health in the UK.

Which leads me onto what even is 'mental health'? It's such a binary way of looking at something, you're either having mental health 'issues' or not, which literally makes no sense whatsoever. We don't say to people that they are either 'healthy' or 'unhealthy', or simply say someone is, 'unfit' or 'fit'. We accept and understand that there is a huge continuum from 'unfit' to 'fit'. Surely then the same can be said for mental health? There is such a fundamental lack of understanding around the language we use for this, to help us grasp what it is - no wonder we don't know what's going on. You can see if you're putting weight on, you can feel if your physical fitness is slipping - these are tactile things. However in the mind, it's not so easy to tell what's going on.

One of the key turning points for me, and as obvious as this sounds, was starting to treat my mental health simply as 'my' health, mind and body as one. As easy as that sounds, it took many many years to arrive at that point, as was the decline in my mental health - it didn't happen over night. What starts out as a concern about something over time became worry, which developed into anxiety, to catastrophising about everything and being almost crippled into inaction by anxiety driven depression. This was a gradual decline over 10+ years, just as with my physical health and fitness. Having been so supremely fit and strong, after 10 years I was at rock bottom and could not see a way back, or what the point of 'back' was.

Like everyone else, I was doing my 22 press ups to raise awareness, retweeting, hash-tagging and telling anyone who would listen that it was 'ok to not be ok', whilst at the same time ensuring not to tell anyone that I was in fact **not ok.**

What does anxiety driven depression look like? It looks like this picture, because a lack of mental health is easily hidden as it can't be seen (apart from being 30lbs overweight as I am in this picture with Amy). It's also actively hidden by those suffering, like me - we become experts at wearing a mask which covers everything, even from those closest to us. The problem with wearing this mask is it also distorts your own world view, as you slip deeper and deeper beneath the waves. So far that you can't see a way back, there's no one to help you back - and what even is the point anyway?

Your reality is hidden from you by this mask, just as it hides what you're going through from those closest to you. The only thing it leaves visible to you behind the mask is the shame, embarrassment and hopelessness that comes with depression. Surely and obviously everyone would be better off without you. The idea that everyone around you would be better off without you makes perfect sense at the time, as ridiculous as that sounds - it is the reality inside your head.

The truth shall set you free, but first it will piss you off
Gloria Steinem

Around 5 years ago I hit rock bottom, I was drinking heavily and self medicating with tramadol to help get me to sleep. I was a walking heart attack waiting to happen, or worse. At 2am one morning I was walking around the area where we live, in the pouring rain, I had to do something as I couldn't lie awake with my heart racing and my mind racing any faster - I realised help wasn't coming. It was then I was able to start forming ideas on how to move forward. Or at least move in a direction regardless. The first thing I did was admit I had a problem, what the problem was like and what if anything made it worse or made it better.

At it's core and what had been coming for many years was my total lack of identity or sense of self. My self esteem was completely anchored to my job, and as I loved my job I thought that was fine. Except my job doesn't or shouldn't define me, so as a self employed person all I was doing was being at the mercy of the shifting sands of work and the money that went with it. The saying that do something you love for work and you'll never 'work' a day in your life is bullshit, because all you do is work all the time, take everything personally, have no boundaries between work/home and take everything personally. This had a massive detrimental effect on me, albeit death by 1000 paper cuts as it takes so many years. I also had a completely unresolved relationship with my military past.

I was so utterly focused on leaving, to make a new life I completely wiped those 9 years from my life. I didn't stay in touch with hardly anyone, didn't tell anyone or acknowledge it in any way. My wife knew next to nothing and my daughter didn't know one detail or even that I had served at all. The reality is ignoring those 9 years was a mistake, there were a huge amount of things to be proud of and ultimately defined me as a person. By ignoring them completely I was throwing the good out with the bad, a load of emotional and mental tools which could serve me well.

I could go a whole day or even days without eating anything, not sleeping, unable to concentrate, short tempered and found no joy or pleasure in anything. Now at rock bottom it was in fact my military past that showed me a possible path out of the hole I was in. Finding myself totally unrecognisable physically and mentally, I looked back on my 25 year old self as something to 'reset' myself to - almost like a 'restore from back up'. I went to see a sports doctor I knew to talk everything I was going through, he was fantastic and pointed me back in the direction of my GP. Whilst I'm sure GP's vary between practices, they receive significant training in mental health and can help. I'm not saying they're able to help everyone, but my GP was certainly able to help me with an SSRI. The stigma around taking any sort of medication was so powerful to me, I resisted using anything for 6 months. The more I talked it through and related it to more mundane things in every day life (if you have a headache you take a tablet) the more it made sense.

The brain is an exceptionally complex biological computer, it's difficult to grasp the reactions that need to happen within it to function. The emotions I was going through create a physical reaction, and the biochemistry was so out of whack after over a decade that I wasn't simply training my wait out of it, You're also not going to 'think' your way out of an emotion, which is why talking is so vital. I'm quick to back myself and trying to focus my mind on this to beat it wasn't working, because it's my own mind.

Training has been key to my mental health. My
mental health is my physical health and vice versa.
They are the same thing to me, and I treat them
as such.

After 6 weeks on a very mild SSRI I was beginning to feel better in myself. My private self was beginning to catch up with character I played to everyone else. I also began to eat a really good healthy diet, and train regularly again. I was 30lbs overweight and had been for years, so with a mind that was thinking more clearly I was able to focus on my health trying to link the two. I also made some significant changes at work, mainly avoiding all the drama triangles. The Drama Triangle - is everywhere, and you probably don't see it. You could be the cause of it, or an unwitting participant in it, the key is recognising it. The drama triangle involves a Persecutor, a Victim and a Saviour. You can initiate a drama triangle by simply asking someone to do something, they then become the victim and need to recruit a saviour which means pulling someone into the 'Drama Triangle'.

I avoid drama triangles at all costs, which is hard because the more you look the more you realise how widespread they are. However recognising them, my role in them and staying the fuck out of them is one of the keys to my personal mental health. Getting dragged into the fuckery of a drama triangle doesn't help anyone, or more importantly me, so I don't play a role in them or initiate one by being the persecutor. Drama triangles are catnip for emotional and mental health dramas and the people that thrive off them, for me they are toxic. Don't mistake this for a mate calling for help, that is a completely different thing. They are not a victim, are not being persecuted, they simply need my help - even if it's just to listen.

As with life there are ups and downs, and I don't think you can 'beat' depression, but you can certainly start to pro-actively deal with it. For veterans suffering with combat stress or transition stress, I think it's something completely different made worse by society, ham fisted approaches by the MoD and the worst of worst - other veterans or serving.

We are our own worst enemies, the toxic BroVet community is something to behold. They will do 22 press ups for suicide, then slate someone for being a snowflake for speaking out. They will be first to rise up against a socialist society whilst at the very same time expecting an entourage of people from all the non profits to give them what they want. The only stigma I've faced is of my own doing via my own ego, I don't think civvies give two fucks about any sort of veteran mental health issue - not because they are jack as fuck, but simply because it's so common in society. My personal experience of civvies when they're confronted with a veteran with PTSD is one of empathy and wanting to help, no judgement or hostility. I'm not saying this is everyone's experience, just what I've seen first hand. That's in direct contrast to how I see veterans and serving deal with someone with PTSD which can be hostile and judgmental, as mentioned probably whilst re-tweeting something about 'please talk to someone'.

No matter how many press ups anyone does, the GP still doesn't have the time or resources to help as they would want to - veteran or not. So let's start helping locally and those we know who need help. Maybe vote for who is going to fund mental health services properly in your area or nationally. Me doing 22 press ups isn't going to help my mate, but the spare room will so he's got a roof over his head when he needs it. We have to get away from what might turn into the cliché of a 'broken soldier', where 'PTSD' is synonymous with a combat veteran about to explode at any moment, because it's us that are perpetuating that. Everyone needs help, some a lot more than others and we can provide that to each other, helping each other and not being twats about it.

Absolutely guaranteed that someone will leave a review on Amazon about how shit this book is, badly written, loads of grammatical errors and how much better 'x' book is and buy that instead. They will blast past the fact we've all contributed voluntarily to collate authentic content to produce a book ourselves, where any profit goes to a veteran charity. Why - because people are fucking bell ends, civilian and veteran alike.

The point of this book and the reason I'm saying this is because everyone is on some sort of journey, and it's very easy to think it's only you with all the negative bullshit that stops people from speaking out. I've been able to use my service as a tool for good to help me find my way back to myself, enabling me to reconnect with the airborne soldier I used to be, and use all of the skills that made me an airborne soldier to tackle life positively. This is not all or nothing, one or the other, as with everything it's a blend - civvies are not going to respond to the Brecon Point, why should they? Using my military self as a base I created a new map to deal with the world in front of me which wasn't 'civilian' or 'veteran' - we're just 'people'.

Over the course of a year I lost 2 1/2 stone, got my fitness back to something resembling my old self with continued support from Amy. I also started attending military occasions like Remembrance Day, eventually being in a place to get the medals out and the old jacket on with unit bullion badge without feeling like some weird walt. From admitting I needed help to the position I'm in now was around 2 years, so this is not an overnight process. It took 10+ years to hit rock bottom, so this wasn't going to be sorted in a few weeks. However each week and each month things got easier and easier to deal with.

I don't think you ever truly beat something like this, just like you're never at supreme physical fitness at all times - but you can stay on top of it and **regain control of your life, and yourself.**

Lee Davies

Unknown DZ, PX4 jump, 1994 or 1995

The Airborne Soldier

Superb fitness is required to build up the body and mind in order to create the total self confidence to overcome the initial fear of leaping into the unknown. Stamina is needed to carry the tortuously heavy loads of equipment and ammunition into battle. Above all, paratroopers need to overcome the opposition even when faced with vastly superior odds, and the endurance to carry on fighting to the bitter end when that is necessary

It is a mixture of these qualities and skills, together with parachuting which creates the thinking solider, who in the process forms a close bond with his comrades.

He knows the capabilities of the men around him, they know and respect him. He is physically and mentally robust, thus is able to handle stress in all its forms. He believes that nothing can stop him, his morale is high, he is self disciplined and totally motivated to win.

Such is the airborne solider.

Thank me for my service?

In full rig at a wedding, it was an opportunity for me to continue to reconcile my military past with the here and now.

My experience is we're our own worst enemies, by far. We shout about how we're misunderstood, civvies don't care, no one is bothered about us. My reality is the group of people I've found to be the most entrenched, intractable, belligerent, judgemental, binary thinking, all or nothing, I'm right you're wrong, echo chamber, cognitive dissonance and straight up hostile - are veterans. The largest group of people waiting and wanting you to fail, other veterans.

This has created the impression to anyone on the outside that veterans are either stoic as fuck superhuman machines that feel no pain or emotions whatsoever, or PTSD sufferers that are about to explode and stab someones face off. Obviously neither is the case in any way.

The intellectual BDSM playground that is social media has fuelled this faster than my missus with a discount code for LuLu Lemon.

We don't have to like each other, or all sit around a camp fire singing hymns together. However if we want to reconcile anything with ourselves and the communities we live in, maybe we should start behaving and treating each other as we would like to be treated in the one community we claim to belong to - the 'veteran' community. This also means if I'm going to wear full rig to a wedding then someone is inevitably going to ask questions, so I should look forward to answering them - otherwise why be stood there in the rig in the first place?

I don't feel like need people to thank me for anything, or feel comfortable when they do. What I did and where I did it had zero impact on them or their lives, it's not like I saved any of them from invading forces, and you could argue they are less safe now because of failed foreign policies over the last 30 years. But I will accept their thanks, and that I served with the best of intentions, which was to defend my country. Whilst defending my country didn't actually happen because everything was about implementing corrupt geopolitical foreign policies, that is not the civvies fault or mine. So rather than project onto them my total dissatisfaction with a lot of what happened and why, I focus on the positives, because there are a lot of them. Not everyone got to do what I did, and civilians are a lot more receptive to the stories than you think.

Thanks for the thanks, I take it from people in the spirit it's intended - because those intentions are good. The dits may seem a bit blah to me, maybe even cringey - but people want to hear them, and when you look at it from their perspective it's understandable why.

If we want to bridge the gap from military to veteran to civilian, we're an ambassador for that process and all of us when we wear the rig.

So please answer the questions, accept the thanks with humility and spin the dits with humour, because that's who we really are.

Don't be a fucking prick about it.

Thanks for taking the time to read this book.

I genuinely hope it helps you in some way. There is
a whole community out there that we are able to
tap into, to reconnect with a tribe, throw bants
around and not be alone. There is a toxic BroVet
community, but that is no different to when we
were in, we carry the same bullshit with us into

civvie street. People trying to out Ally each other, out stoic each other or being jack as fuck. Yet we're very quick to slate civilians and their lack of understanding, when we really need to look at ourselves first.

Connecting myself to the good bits of my military experience to my present self has been key to restoring my sense of self and who I am.

If you are struggling for whatever reason, then please please say something, anything. Once you remove the mask and reveal yourself, so many things open up for you and the fears about judgement don't materialise, not from those that matter.

I couldn't have done this book without the help of everyone who contributed, who did so without hesitation. We all want to help each other, we are all brothers & sisters.

Thanks again

Daz

NUNQUAM NON PARATUS

Juno Beach, Normandy, 6th June 2019

THE VETERAN
COLLECTIVE

Printed in Great Britain
by Amazon